The Snows of Yesteryear

J. Norman Collie, Mountaineer

William C. Taylor

Holt, Rinehart and Winston of Canada, Limited   Toronto ● Montreal

Copyright© 1973 by Holt, Rinehart and Winston of Canada,
Limited

ISBN 0-03-929953-8

Library of Congress Catalogue Card Number: 73-14100

Printed in Canada

1   2   3   4   5   77 76   75   74   73

PREFACE

My fascination with the enigmatic figure of J. Norman Collie developed over many years. It was in Lillian Gest's account of the early history of the region around Lake O'Hara in the Canadian Rockies that I first came across his name. He was, it seems, one of the first men to scale the peaks around the lake. Then a year or two later, while reading K. M. Herrlig-koffer's book *Nanga Parbat*, I learned that the initial attempt on this fearsome peak was undertaken in 1895 by A.F. Mummery, G. Hastings, and J. N. Collie. Was it not likely that this was the same Collie mentioned by Lillian Gest? The proof came a year later when Maryalice H. Stewart at the Archives of the Canadian Rockies in Banff, greeting my inquiries concerning Collie with her wonderful enthusiasm, directed me to his books, articles, letters and photographs. As time went by, it became obvious that Collie was no "obscure professor of chemistry" as I had at first supposed, but a fascinating character out of the late Victorian era who had excelled at science, mountaineering, exploration, geography, photography, art and whatever else he turned his hand to. Most of all he was a prolific writer of considerable skill who wrote two books on mountaineering and numerous articles in alpine journals. His letters, moreover, had been preserved by his nieces and several correspondents in North America. As if this was not enough there were still people alive who remembered Collie. This, by the way, is part of the fascination of the history of Western Canada: that what today lingers on as the memories of a few people, will tomorrow be history, and that many such memories will be irretrievably lost if not gathered in time.

Two short biographical sketches have been written about Collie; one appeared in *Six Great Mountaineers* by Ronald Clark and the other in *Because It's There* by Walter Unsworth. I was, however, most surprised to learn that no one had undertaken a full-length study of Collie who, for various reasons, had fallen into obscurity. His survival until the age of eighty-three ensured that he outlived all his climbing friends and most of his contemporaries. His death in 1942, at the height of the Second World War went all but unnoticed, except for a few obituaries in the mountain-eering journals then struggling against shortages of paper. Besides, after the war, mountaineering in Britain rapidly reached a level which far exceeded the greatest moments of the Golden Age of Edward Whymper or the Silver Age of Mummery, Hastings, Slingsby and Collie. However, now that we have had thirty years in which to accustom ourselves to the spectacular triumphs of modern mountaineering, it is perhaps not inap-propriate to take a nostalgic look back to the time, about seventy years ago, when J. Norman Collie was one of the four greatest climbers in the world.

ACKNOWLEDGEMENTS

One of the great pleasures of working on this book was the kind help and cooperation that I received from so many people. I am particularly grateful to Professor Collie's two nieces, Mrs. Susan Benstead, of Cambridge, England, and Mrs. Nora Holmes, of Masterton, New Zealand; to Maryalice H. Stewart, Director of the Archives of the Canadian Rockies and her staff who started me off on the whole project and periodically instilled me with fresh enthusiasm; to Dr. J. Monroe Thorington of Philadelphia whose foresight preserved the Collie-Thompson correspondence, who provided me with background information from his vast fund of knowledge of the Canadian Rockies and who helped correct the manuscript; to Sheilagh S. Jameson, Archivist of the Glenbow-Alberta Institute who made available the correspondence between Collie and Tom Wilson of Banff; to Mr. B. H. Humble of Aviemore, Scotland who helped greatly with information about Collie and John Mackenzie in Skye and allowed me to quote from his books; to Mrs. Charles E. Scribner for permission to reproduce extracts from Collie's correspondence with her father Mr. C. S. Thompson; to Ian S. Campbell proprietor of Sligachan Hotel, Skye; to James M. Lee of the Kings House Hotel, Glencoe, Scotland, and to Valerie Wilson of the Wastwater Hotel, Wasdale Head; to the Registrars of the Universities of Glasgow, Belfast, Liverpool and St. Andrews; to P. McNab, Shire Clerk of Collie, Western Australia; to the State Archivist, Perth, Western Australia for providing microfilm of the correspondence between Dr. Alexander Collie and his brother George Collie in Aberdeen; to Dorothy Pilley (Mrs. I.A. Richards) of Cambridge, Massachusetts, for providing personal reminiscence of Professor Collie; to the late Jim Simpson for his personal recollections of Collie and Fred Stephens; to Alan Cooke, curator of manuscripts at the Scott Polar Research Institute; to T. S. Blakeney, secretary of the Mount Everest Foundation; to Robert Inglis of the Scottish Mountaineering Club; and to Miss J. A. Callander, the librarian, and E. F. Johnston, the secretary, of the Cairngorm Club in Aberdeen for providing hard-to-find copies of their journal and for drawing my attention to the story of the "Big Grey Man of Ben Macdhui."

The following very kindly gave permission to reproduce published material: the Scottish Mountaineering Club; the Royal Geographical Society; Longman Group Limited; Macmillan and Company Limited; St. Martin's Press; Macmillan Publishing Company; Thomas Nelson and Sons; G.P. Putnam's Sons; the Cairngorm Club; the Alpine Club; and Mr. B.H. Humble.

Lastly my special thanks go to Lillian Wonders for help with geographical material and preparation of maps; to Mrs. Vi Love for help in typing; to Kay Stewart who with quiet understanding helped revise the manuscript; and to the publishers for their editorial help.

CONTENTS

Chapter One
Collie the Man

Collie the Man

The summer traveller who stands on the shores of Lake Louise in Banff National Park and gazes at the mighty cliffs of Mount Victoria and Mount Lefroy may hear a distant yodel, the triumphant call of a climber who has scaled the heights. A short walk to the end of the lake, a hike up the Plain of the Six Glaciers, and there the traveller will discover a forbidding valley ascending to the south. Known as the "Death Trap," this evil cleft, a gathering place for avalanches, leads to the Abbot Pass 9000 feet above sea level. The routes to the mountaintops, Victoria on the right and Lefroy on the left, start from this pass where a stone hut was erected by Swiss guides in 1922. Mount Victoria was first conquered in August 1897 by a climbing party led by a British chemist and mountaineer, Professor J. Norman Collie.

At mile 77 of the Banff-Jasper Highway, our traveller will arrive at the Columbia Ice Field, centre of the greatest accumulation of ice in the Rocky Mountains. The most accessible part of the Ice Field is the Athabasca Glacier, which may be viewed from the comfort of the chalet, or traversed in the safety of a snowmobile. To the left of the Glacier rises an impressive snow-covered mountain, Mount Athabasca, first climbed on August 18, 1898, by Professor J. Norman Collie.

These two climbs were only a small part of Collie's exploits in the Canadian Rockies. During six pioneering expeditions in the years 1897-1911, he made twenty-one first ascents and named at least thirty peaks. The survey maps which resulted from his explorations were used for more than twenty years. The publicity which the Rockies received in his book *Climbs and Exploration in the Canadian Rockies* (written with Hugh E. M. Stutfield), in lectures, and in articles for mountaineering journals undoubtedly contributed to their rapidly-growing popularity among mountain climbers in the early 1900's.

Before launching his attacks upon the mountains of the New World, Collie had served a ten-year apprenticeship among the peaks of the Old. Unlike most British climbers of his day, Collie learned his climbing in Britain rather than in the Alps. When he did reach the Alps, it was to climb with some of the foremost mountaineers of the time—A. F. Mummery, Geoffrey Hastings, and Cecil Slingsby. This group initiated the practice of scaling peaks by more difficult routes, thus raising climbing standards, and of climbing without guides. As a member of Mummery's Himalayan expedition of 1895, only the third serious assault on those formidable peaks, Collie reached a height of between 19,000 and 20,000 feet, a rare achievement at that time.

One of the reasons for Collie's remarkable achievements lay in his ancestry. The Collie family, originally Irish, had moved to Aberdeenshire in the days of Oliver Cromwell. This Celtic strain may have accounted for the roving streak in many of the family, such as Collie's grand-uncle Alexander Collie who, after receiving his medical degree at Edinburgh, entered the Royal Navy. Little is known of his career until he embarked as surgeon of H.M.S. *Blossom,* which under the command of Captain (later Sir) F. W. Beechey, R.N., cooperated with Lieutenant John Franklin in the latter's second expedition to the Arctic in 1824-25. The *Blossom* sailed ahead of Franklin's ship, laying down depots of food at various points in the Arctic to supplement the provisions carried by Franklin. After completing this assignment, the *Blossom* sailed around the world, visiting Mexico, California, the Aleutians and many other places. On the voyage, Alexander Collie, who was a keen naturalist, had a Mexican magpie-jay named after him, the "Calacitta Colliei." Throughout the voyage, Collie wrote a naturalist's journal and a "Journal of Events." The latter, according to the usual rule, was handed in to the Admiralty at the end of the voyage. Unfortunately Captain Beechey, who also wanted to write up the expedition, took exception to certain passages in Collie's Journal, and the Admiralty impounded the documents until the two officers could reach agreement. Collie's Journal was never released.

Shortly after his return to England, Dr. Collie was appointed surgeon to H.M.S. *Sulphur*, which sailed with Captain Stirling and a party of soldiers and settlers for the Swan River in Western Australia. After their arrival at Freemantle on June 8, 1829, Collie and Lieutenant Preston, each in charge of a whaleboat, were sent off to examine the southwest coast. Collie discovered two rivers, named by Stirling the Preston and the Collie, upon whose banks the town of Collie was later erected, and later a third river, presumably named by Collie himself the Margaret, after his niece. Dr. Collie settled in Australia, where he died on November 5, 1835. His estate, including a house and land in Perth, was left in equal part to his brothers James and George. The latter was J. Norman Collie's grandfather. The letters which Alexander wrote to George were preserved, and one hundred years later, his grandnephew Norman, with a fine sense of history, arranged for their deposition with the State Archives of Western Australia.

George's son John Collie, a member of the family cotton firm, married Selina Mary, the third daughter of Henry Winkworth, a silk merchant. Mrs. Susan Benstead, Norman Collie's niece, recalls that her grandmother Selina was a fine musician, a most delightful person, and much more human than her three sisters. The Winkworths were an artistic and literary family, personal friends of James Anthony Froude, Charles Kingsley, the Gaskells and the Martineaus. The youngest daughter, Catherine, translated hymns from the German language; her sister Susanna edited a posthumous collection of her letters. A social reformer like others of her circle, Susanna did pioneering work for many years in Clifton and Bristol on the provision of model dwellings for working-class people. After Catherine's death she replaced her sister as a member of the council of Cheltenham Ladies' College, where her nephew Norman held his first post.

There was a precedent for Collie's interest in mountain climbing, as well as his taste for art and literature, in the Winkworth family. His Uncle Stephen was elected to the Alpine Club, then only seven years old, in 1861. It was an exclusive organization, limiting its membership to the upper and professional classes, but on occasion opening its ranks to men who had acquired position or wealth. Stephen made many climbs in the Alps, including Mont Blanc, Monte Rosa and the Jungfrau, accompanied by his wife at a time when women were hardly welcomed into the ranks of climbers. The relationship between young Norman Collie and his Uncle Stephen was very close, and during the years of financial troubles the uncle helped out with an annual allowance. He died in 1886, the year that Norman began his mountaineering career.

Norman Collie's ancestry is of considerable interest because it helps to explain many of his outstanding characteristics and the striking personality with which he was unquestionably endowed. From the Collies he inherited the inbred caution of the Scot, the apparently ascetic nature, the dry sense of humour, the quaint old-fashioned mysticism and the wandering instincts which have sent many a Celt to the distant regions of the earth.

From the Winkworths he inherited a love of beauty, a natural skill in writing, an artistic taste exemplified in his collection of beautiful works of art, and from Stephen Winkworth he must surely have learned of the challenge of the mountains. Collie's photographs suggest the contradictory nature of his personality. The long, bony, unsmiling face contrasts strongly with the sensuous mouth. His face is full of character, stern and at times unfriendly. Yet his eyes have a kindly look and it seems more than likely that brought up as he was in a large family circle, he was a friendly man although he took good care to hide this along with his natural shyness behind a stern exterior. He was selective in his friendships, but once a friendship had been established it remained for life.

John Norman Collie, the second of four sons, was born on September 10, 1859, at Alderly Edge, Manchester. Norman and his older brother Henry were close companions throughout boyhood, sharing the same tutors and common interests such as fishing, bird nesting, tree climbing and hill walking. In most of these activities Norman appears to have been the leader.

When Norman was six years old his father retired to a small shooting estate at Glassel on lower Deeside not far from Aberdeen, where he could indulge himself in fishing and shooting. There the two older boys doubtless had time to spare from their private lessons to explore the countryside around them. Lower Deeside is a most attractive region with rolling, well-wooded hills sloping down to the gently flowing Dee. To the west lie the outlying foothills of the Grampians around Banchory with the first promise of mysterious mountains lying beyond. Collie believed that he first acquired his love for the hills when, as a boy of eight, he spent long days wandering over the Hill of Fare. As an old man of eighty he still recalled its magic: "It was on a perfect summer day; all the flowers were there to show that summer had come and the birds were everywhere busy with their nests. At the edge of Glassel woods, I found a willow wren's nest full of eggs. From the top of the hill I had my first view of Lochnagar. The Corrichie burn was still running red in memory of that fierce fight in byegone days."

In 1870 the family left Glassel and went to live in Clifton, near Bristol. Here Norman, although far removed from the hills of Scotland, managed to find excitement in climbing the dangerous cliffs of the Clifton Gorge. He first went to school at Windlesham in Surrey, transferring in 1873 to Charterhouse, then as now one of the leading public schools in England. But his days at an expensive school, with its valuable social advantages,

J. Norman Collie seated, his elder brother Henry, and mother, c. 1863 were cut short by the financial disaster which overtook his father in 1875.

The origin of the Collie fortune is not known, but by the middle of the nineteenth century the family firm was one of the biggest cotton importers in Britain. It is likely that old George Collie founded the enterprise. Once a tenant farmer in Aberdeenshire, he had in later life moved to a large home in Aberdeen. The inheritance which he received from his brother Alexander probably helped. Two of his seven children, Alexander and John (Norman Collie's father), worked for the firm. During the American Civil War, their ships ran the blockade and supplied the South with food and ammunition; in return they were paid in raw cotton. British officers used to apply for leave with the unspoken intention of commanding these ships, for the profits made on each successful run were spectacular. When Sherman went "marching through Georgia" he burned about one million pounds' worth of Collie cotton waiting to be loaded, a crippling blow from which the firm never recovered. Alexander Collie, an unscrupulous man, thought he could recoup their fortunes by raising two loans simultaneously on the same lot of cotton. Unfortunately the compensation he was expecting from the United States Government never materialized, and when the loans were called the firm went bankrupt. Many smaller firms were ruined along with them. Alexander left hurriedly for the United States and remained there until he died. His wife, the very beautiful Flora MacNeill (descendant of Prince Charles Edward's Flora Macdonald) reassumed her maiden name, and a son later moved to Canada.

At the time of the crash, John Collie, who played no part in the shady dealings, severed all personal connections with the firm, although he did not withdraw his money to avoid creating further difficulties. Some time later he invested his small remaining capital in a paper mill in Kent, but this venture also failed. The family was thus reduced from considerable wealth to impoverishment over a period of a few years. They were saved from·absolute poverty only by a small inheritance belonging to Selina Collie and by the efforts of her brother Stephen Winkworth, who paid Norman Collie a yearly allowance of one hundred pounds during his student years.

From Charterhouse Norman was transferred to Clifton College, Bristol as a day pupil. His performance as a student of the classics was so poor that he was asked to leave the school, and it was not until he took up the study of science at University College in Bristol that he discovered where his real interest lay. Under the guidance of Professor E. A. Letts he studied chemistry on a scholarship, and finally completed his training at

Würzburg University, Germany, where he obtained the Ph.D. degree in 1884.

Many letters to his mother from this period of his life have been preserved. The recurrent theme is his strained financial circumstances. Thus on December 8, 1882, he wrote: "I got your letter and I am awfully sorry to hear how hard up you are. I am still worse or I never should have asked you for money. I have got nothing at all and Richardson has only 8 shillings (marks) and I owe him some money. So in four days we shall starve. I hope you will be able to beg borrow or steal some money." Fortunately his mother and Uncle Stephen rallied to the cause and Norman had money to spend in time for Christmas. But Germany was not all poverty and hard work. On August 24, 1883, he wrote to describe a happy day's outing with a friend to Swinsenberg Castle overlooking the Neckar River.

> About 4 o'clock we started to go 30 or 35 miles to Heidelberg in our canoes. We took 3 hours getting to Neckarsteinach and two more getting home to Heidelberg. It was nearly pitch dark when we got to the rapids above Heidelberg and I thought that I was really going to have been upset, for the canoe was turned right round at the beginning and as we were amongst large waves and the stream running 6 or 7 miles an hour, and I had shipped a couple of seas, it really was rather risky. Then again we could not see the arches of the bridge and if we had run against one of the buttresses the canoe would have gone to pieces like matchwood. I was very glad to get safe home and not send the canoe to the bottom.

After completing his studies in Germany, Collie was appointed science lecturer at Cheltenham Ladies' College, a post he thoroughly disliked, although he stuck it out for two years. In 1887 he moved to London as demonstrator in the chemical laboratories at University College, where he worked with Sir William Ramsay. Thereafter he steadily progressed in the field of organic chemistry. In the chapters that follow, Collie will be seen exclusively as a mountaineer, and it is important to remember that in between his many famous exploits, he pursued a long and distinguished career as a scientist of considerable eminence. More will be said about his scientific achievements in the final chapter.

Collie's artistic taste found an outlet even in his scientific work. During his investigations into the effects of high energy electric discharges on gases at low temperatures, a colleague said to him, "Collie, I truly believe that you are far more interested in the colours of the discharges than in the striking phenomena you are recording." Outside of his work, his artis-

Dighton's Art Studio CHELTENHAM.

Collie, April 1886, the year he started climbing

tic taste found expression in painting, photography, and writing. His close friend Colin B. Phillip, R.S.W. remarked that his pupil bid fair to beat him in water colours. He produced, for example, a particularly fine water colour of his long-time guide, companion, and friend, John Mackenzie of Skye. His photography was of an extremely high standard for the time, and his two books and many of his mountaineering articles are illustrated by his own photographs. His finest black and white photographs are in his book *Climbing on the Himalaya and Other Mountain Ranges.* He was a pioneer in the field of colour photography and colour processing, in which his scientific knowledge was used to good advantage. As a writer, Collie was at his best describing the beauty of the mountain scenery through which he travelled.

Collie was also a connoisseur and collector of note, particularly knowledgeable in the wide field of Chinese and Japanese porcelain, ivories, bronzes and embroideries, about which he published several articles. He collected rare editions with beautiful types and bindings. To a degree almost unfair amongst collectors, his scientific knowledge complemented his artistic judgement. He could buy precious stones on sight at sales or auctions, and at bargain prices, since his expert touch told him as much of their nature by weight and feel, as his eye by their colour. He delighted in the production of glorious colours from jewels by bombarding them with rays in his laboratory.

A confirmed bachelor, Collie lived in a suite of rooms in Campden Grove until the house was pulled down. Later he lived in a house in Gower Street, surrounded by all his treasures in apparent chaos. He shared this house with Robert S. Cox, a solicitor, who provided the lovely old furniture and silver that made their admirable dinner parties aesthetically as well as gastronomically celebrated. Yet, in spite of the chaos, everything in sight—china, jade, metals, books and paintings—was so arranged as to pick up and repeat colour or lighting in a scheme designed for his own pleasure. Here he lived, something of a recluse, except for company of his own choosing. His dinners were celebrated for the quality of the food and particularly the drink, as he was an authority on wines, especially vintage clarets. To these dinners he might invite students or junior colleagues but more likely his friends such as the medieval scholar W. P. Ker, the painter Colin Phillip, and fellow mountaineers, Hugh Stutfield, Sir Francis Younghusband, Major Charles Granville Bruce or Cecil Slingsby. At such times the discussion might range over problems of exploration, philosophy, art or literature with perhaps short showings of his beautiful slides to illustrate a point or the passing round of one of his treasures to introduce some new idea into the talk.

Like quite a few scientists Collie was less interested in human beings than in ideas, objects or colour. This is obvious from his writings which hardly ever describe people or his own impressions of them. Only two individuals are mentioned affectionately, and those were both guides— Fred Stephens in Canada, "one of the best fellows it has ever been our good fortune to meet," and John Mackenzie. He was not easily approachable except upon the ground of a common interest, but one suspects that this was largely due to a combination of a natural shyness, the inborn caution of the "canny Scot," and the lack of the mellowing effect of female companionship. In spite of his aloofness he had many life-long friends with whom he pursued one or more of his interests, but especially mountaineering. There is no evidence that he seriously contemplated matrimony at any time although he expressed envy of his friend Thompson on the occasion of his marriage. He did climb in the Alps with the remarkable Lily Bristow, but she was part of a sparkling group of young people who surrounded the Mummerys. He had three young nieces who visited him from time to time, and a housekeeper to care for his rooms, but apart from this and a great devotion to his mother, there was no female companionship in his life.

To younger men with similar interests in science, art, or mountaineering he could be generous and helpful. He started Dr. A. M. Kellas off on a productive career of Himalayan exploration. Convinced of the outstanding qualities of the young Alpinist and subsequent Greenland explorer Gino Watkins, Collie obtained from the Royal Geographical Society the financial support which allowed Watkins to commence his Arctic explorations in 1930. William Garden described how one fine morning he had the misfortune to be hanging around the hotel door at Sligachan in Skye, feeling annoyed because his climbing boots had been burned while drying, and he had been reduced to wearing ordinary shoes. Collie spotted his annoyance at once and saying that Garden must not loaf around on such a fine morning, promptly invited him on a climb on the Am Bhasteir face of Knight's Peak. Collie proved not so obliging, however, when Willy Merkl, a German climber, asked for an introduction. Between the blonde, efficient, hustling young modernist with his card neatly printed as "Leader of the Nanga Parbat Expedition" (and later its victim) and the scholarly artist, member of the first party to attack that peak, there was a gap of time and temperament which proved unbridgeable. The startled young German was escorted from the room while Collie was still discoursing remotely to space about the optical miracle represented by the first character of the Chinese alphabet.

In appearance Collie was lean and erect, with a length of arm and leg which greatly contributed to his skill as a rock climber. His features were long and pointed with sombre eyes, a serious look and hair which hung lank and greying. In later life he closely resembled the pictures of Sherlock Holmes which were just appearing in the *Strand Magazine* at that time. His favourite apparel was a tweed jacket with matching knickerbocker trousers, a waistcoat, collar and tie and long woollen socks which on horseback or mountain climbing were well wrapped in puttees. In most of his photographs and in one oil painting he holds a pipe from which he was never long separated. He was an inveterate smoker of pipe and cigars, ignorning all advice from his friends about the possible harmful effects of tobacco. His students claimed that the only time he smoked a cigarette was when he was filling a pipe. One of his nieces, Mrs. Susan Benstead, remembers visiting him in Gower Street where, clad in a thick Jaeger dressing gown over a Highland homespun suit, he would be seated in front of a blazing fire. All the windows would be tightly closed and the room filled with a dense cloud of tobacco smoke. His niece was always astonished that, given these habits, he was able to spend six months each year in the open air in all kinds of weather. The more advice his friends gave him, the more ostentatious was his habit of stopping to light up his pipe before tackling a difficult pitch on the mountainside. He always believed that his pipe helped him to survive great hardship on Nanga Parbat. In spite of his gaunt silver-grey appearance which suggested frailty and senescence, he was never seriously ill and possessed great powers of endurance. In the Himalaya, for example, he was much tougher than Mummery or Hastings. The only indisposition he ever confessed to was indigestion from the appalling food and weakness from altitude sickness on the Nanga Parbat expedition, which also affected his companions. It is known however that he suffered from migraine headaches, an affliction shared with his mother and brother. He remained erect, agile, and physically fit into his eighties. Besides his mountain climbing and fishing, he played golf on courses all over the world from St. Andrews to an improvised course amongst the stately pines of the Himalayan Mountains.

Collie displayed little interest in politics or in the turbulent times through which he lived. Born three years after the end of the Crimean War, and one year after the Indian Mutiny, he grew to manhood as a series of

Collie with his art treasures at Gower Street

frontier wars established the British Empire in the late Victorian era. The nearest he came to war was in 1895 when the expedition to Nanga Parbat visited the northwest frontier of India, shortly after a border conflict had been settled. There Collie and his companions met one of the officers in charge of a field gun battery which had participated in the relief of Chitral. The Boer War was mentioned briefly in one of his books, as not only the trail guides but also the pack ponies from the Canadian Rockies had participated in that conflict. The wars of his early manhood were fought almost exclusively by professional soldiers, and soldiers in those days were not mountaineers. The one notable exception (Major C. G. Bruce) will be introduced in a later chapter. At fifty-five years of age Collie was too old to serve in the First World War; when the Second World War broke out he withdrew from London to the Island of Skye and never returned. He was essentially a man of peace who was fortunate enough to live at a time when personal involvement in war was entirely voluntary.

This then was J. Norman Collie, the man who year after year set out from Campden Grove or Gower Street, usually during the summer months, but sometimes at Christmas or Easter, to explore the mountain world. Unlike other men, who as time went by found their once exclusive devotion to the mountains shared by family and other ties, Collie alone remained to the end wholly and passionately entranced by the lure of the peaks. It is for his achievements in this realm that we best remember him.

Chapter Two
The British Isles

The British Isles

Nowhere in the British Islands are there any rock climbs to be compared with those in Skye, measure them by what standard you will, length, variety, or difficulty. Should anyone doubt this, let him some fine morning walk up from the foot of Coruisk to the rocky slabs at the foot of Sgurr a'Ghreadaidh. There he will see bare grey rocks rising out from the heather not 500 feet above the level of the loch, and these walls, ridges, and towers of weather-worn gabbro stretch with hardly a break to the summit of the mountain, 2800 feet above him. Measured on the map it is only half a mile, but that half-mile will tax his muscles; he must climb up gullies that the mountain torrents have worn out of the precipices, and over slabs of rock sloping down into space at an angle that makes hand-hold necessary as well as foot-hold; he must creep out round edges on the faces of perpendicular cliffs, only to find that after all the perpendicular cliff must be scaled before he can win back again to the ridge that is to lead to the topmost peak.[1]

The only place to which Collie gave his heart, first and last, was the Island of Skye. Here in 1886, on a day when the weather was fine but the fishing poor, twenty-seven-year-old Collie explored the mountains for the first time. Scrambling up into the Coir'a'Bhasteir he watched two skilled climbers making a new ascent on the fourth pinnacle of Sgurr nan Gillean. "Hundreds of feet above me, on what appeared to me to be rocks as steep as the walls of a house, they moved slowly backwards and forwards, but always getting higher, till they finally reached the summit. I knew nothing about climbing, and it seemed to me perfectly marvellous that human beings should be able to do such things." A few days later, with his brother Henry's company and directions from the guide John Mackenzie, Collie succeeded in climbing his first mountain, Am Basteir (the Executioneer). Thereafter he returned to Skye year after year, interrupting his visits only for expeditions to the Alps, the Himalaya, the Canadian Rockies, the Lofotens and short visits to other mountains in the British Isles. When he grew too weak to climb he came back to Skye to fish, and finally to die.

Mountaineering in Skye is centred on the Black Cuillin, a compact range of mountains, about eight miles in length, arranged in a horseshoe around a wild mountain tarn named Loch Coruisk. The main range is made up of twenty-one peaks, most of them over 3000 feet and none below 2500 feet. To the east of Loch Coruisk and guarding the southern approaches to Glen Sligachan are three subsidiary peaks. The Cuillin may not be high by the standards of other mountain ranges, but rising steeply as they do from the sea, they offer no easy way up. The rock gabbro is of a kind unique in the British Isles for its hard crystalline highly abrasive structure; its many protrusions offer excellent handholds and adhesiveness second to none. In fact so excellent is the quality of this rock that many experts consider the surface too easy for beginners to learn rock climbing technique on, as they may acquire a false sense of security. In certain areas smooth slabs of basalt offer fewer holds and are dangerously slippery when wet, as is often the case. The true challenge of the Cuillin, however, lies not in the quality of its rock but in its fantastic mixture of exposed faces, chimneys, traverses, buttresses, towers and superb ridges with wonderful views over deep-cut valleys, the green lochs and the blue sea. For Collie, the fascination of the Cuillin lay in their mystery, a quality which always appealed to him: "The individuality of the Coolin² is not seen in their summits, which are often ugly, but in the colour of the rocks, the atmosphere effects, the relative largeness and harmony of the details compared with the actual size of the mountains, and most of all in the mountain mystery that wraps them round: not the mystery of clearness such as is seen in the Alps and Himalaya, where range after range recedes into the infinite distance till the white snow peaks cannot be distinguished from the clouds, but in the obscure and secret beauty born of the mists, the rain, and the sunshine in a quiet untroubled land, no longer vexed by the more rude and violent manifestations of the active powers of nature."³

The twenty-four peaks of the Cuillin all have Gaelic names; many of these such as Sgurr na h-Uamha (Peak of the cave), Sgurr an Fheadain (Peak of the water-pipe), Sgurr-Dearg (the red Peak) are descriptive of the mountain's appearance. Four of the summits, however, are named after climbers, an unusual mark of esteem in Scotland. Sgurr Thormaid is named for Norman Collie; Sgurr Mhic Coinnich for his longtime guide John Mackenzie; Sgurr Thearlaich (Peak of Charles) for Charles Pilking-

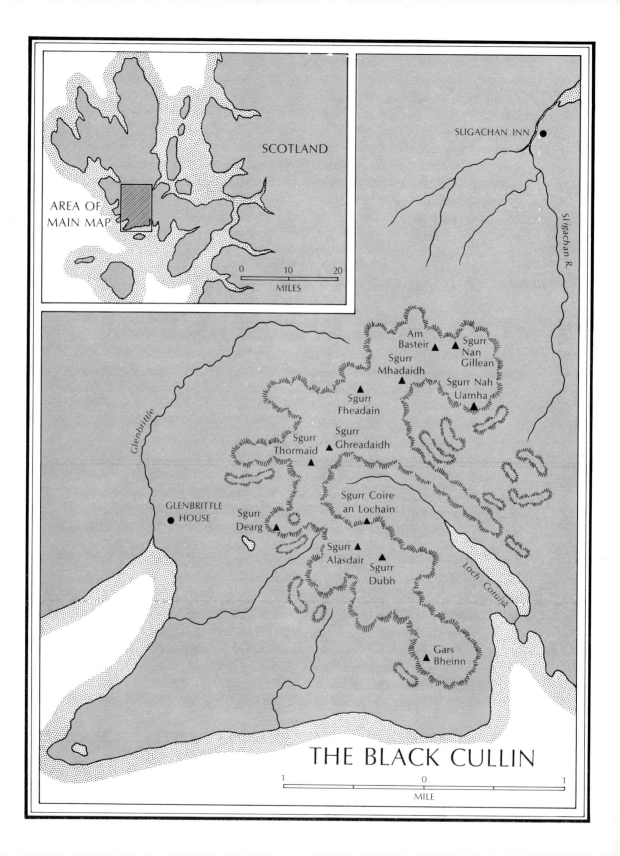

SCOTLAND

AREA OF
MAIN MAP

0   10   20
MILES

SLIGACHAN INN ●

Sligachan R.

Am
Basteir ▲ ▲ Sgurr
Nan
Gillean
Sgurr
Mhadaidh ▲
Sgurr Nah
Uamha
Sgurr ▲
Fheadain ▲

Sgurr
Thormaid ▲ Sgurr ▲
Ghreadaidh

Glenbrittle

GLENBRITTLE ●
HOUSE

Sgurr Coire
an Lochain
Sgurr
Dearg ▲ ▲

Sgurr ▲
Alasdair ▲
Sgurr
Dubh

Loch Coruisk

Gars ▲
Bheinn

THE BLACK CULLIN

1   0   1
MILE

ton, a famous Victorian climber; and Sgurr Alasdair for Sheriff Alexander Nicholson, a pioneer mountaineer in the area.

When Collie first visited Skye, John Mackenzie was the ghillie at Sligachan Inn. Mackenzie had been born in 1856 on a small farm at Sconser, three miles away. B. H. Humble in his delightful book *The Cuillin of Skye* describes how one evening in 1929 he and a friend arrived footsore and weary in the village of Sconser and were directed to the small stone cottage of John Mackenzie. Here they were given a room for the night and invited to partake of food as well. During the meal Humble noticed in a corner of the room a large pile of Alpine Club journals which seemed quite out of place in such a remote corner of Skye.

They were sitting outside the cottage afterwards enjoying the evening sunshine, when down the road towards them strode a grand old man with the easy swinging gait of a veteran hill walker. John Mackenzie, for he it was, wore a baggy ancient tweed suit of plus fours, with capacious pockets, a white handkerchief in the breast pocket, a shirt, tie, and waistcoat. His weather-beaten features were partly hidden by a flowing white beard complete with moustache and sideburns, and his eyes were shaded by a deerstalker hat decorated with fishing flies. On his feet he wore a sturdy pair of mountaineering boots and in his hand he carried some trout, for he had just returned from a day spent fishing in Loch Fada with Professor Collie. Mackenzie, with the characteristic courtesy of the true west highland gentleman, invited the two younger men into his cottage to sit by the kitchen fire. There they talked of climbing and were much encouraged by Mackenzie's assurance that Sgurr Alasdair, the highest peak of them all, was not much more than a walk. He showed them mountain photographs, of which he had many, and gave them much useful advice. He appeared to be an expert on the Cuillin, and this was all the more remarkable, as any other crofter in Skye would have been full of tales of the dangers of the mountains.

It was only when Humble returned to Glasgow and learned more about the occupant of the lonely cottage in Skye that he realized he had met "the only mountain guide of Swiss calibre that Britain had ever produced, and who that day had been in the company of a world-famous mountaineer, the two of them having long years ago ushered in the Golden Age of climbing in Skye!"[4]

The friendship between John Mackenzie and Collie was something very special, lasting as it did from 1886 until the guide's death in 1933. In the extremely class-conscious, highly privileged Victorian world it was

unusual for a "gentleman" to establish close friendships outside his immediate circle. It was a measure of Collie's deep-seated and often carefully hidden humanity that he should establish two such enduring friendships, one with Fred Stephens, the Canadian packer and trail guide, and the other with John Mackenzie. Their friendship was strengthened by the natural wisdom and rugged independence, as well as the considerable skills, of this man of Skye. Collie, who seldom in his writings tried to describe, much less analyse, the people with whom he climbed, had this to say about Mackenzie:

He is the only real British climbing guide that has ever existed. Neither the Lake District nor north Wales has produced one. His great love of the mountains, his keen pleasure in all the beauties of the Cuillin never fails, whether it is a distant view of the mountains, or a sunset fading away behind the outer Hebrides, or the great slabs of gabbro bending over into space, or a still pool of clear water reflecting the rowan bushes and the peaks beyond, or the autumn colours on the rolling moors backed by the hills and the sea - all these do not pass him by unnoticed. He understands not only the joy of a hard climb but can also appreciate the marvels a beautiful mountain world is perpetually offering to one.[5]

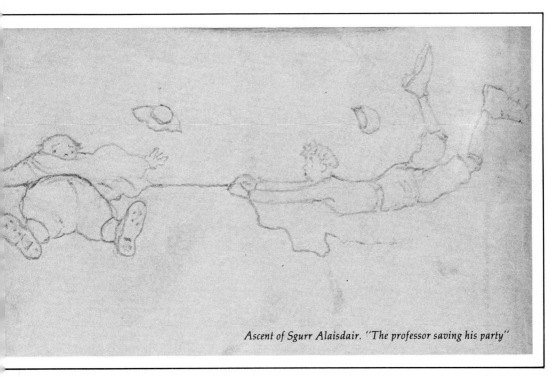

Ascent of Sgurr Alaisdair. "The professor saving his party"

It is interesting to speculate on the development of the climbing skills of Collie and Mackenzie. Three years older than Collie, Mackenzie first climbed Sgurr nan Gillean at the age of ten and made the first ascent of Sgurr a' Ghreadaidh with a Mr. Tribe at the age of fourteen. He accompanied the Pilkington brothers when they climbed the Inaccessible Pinnacle of Sgurr Dearg in 1880, although he did not join them on the summit for that first ascent. It is quite possible that he climbed the Inaccessible Pinnacle alone in 1881, by the slightly easier east ridge and scaled the more difficult west side in 1886 and again in 1887. By 1889 it was possible for Clinton Dent, an eminent climber, to write that Mackenzie "may be without hesitation recommended most strongly as a guide. It is very easy to mistake the way in bad weather and his local knowledge is invaluable. In addition he is a capital climber, takes great interest in all modern refinements of new routes and variations, and is an excellent companion."

By the time Collie began climbing, Mackenzie had accumulated about sixteen years of experience in the Cuillin, much of it with the leading climbers of the day. Collie on his very first climb was guided by Mackenzie's friendly advice, and shortly thereafter he was probably initiated into the techniques of rock climbing and route finding. But whereas Mackenzie never climbed outside the Cuillin, Collie progressed at a phenomenal rate to become within a few years one of the leading British climbers of his generation, familiar not only with the mountains of Britain, but also with the Alps, the Himalaya, the Lofotens and the Canadian Rockies. It is likely that Collie in his turn passed on his new found skills to his friend. Together they made a formidable team in the Cuillin, both expert cragsmen and skilled route finders, and Mackenzie an unrivalled master of the mountains in all kinds of weather, such as Collie has described:

> . . . when the wild Atlantic storms sweep across the mountains; when the streams gather in volume, and the bare rock faces are streaked with foam of a thousand waterfalls; when the wind shrieks amongst the rock pinnacles, and the sky, loch, and hill-side is one dull grey, the Coolin can be savage and dreary indeed; perhaps the clouds towards evening may break, then the torn masses of vapour, tearing in mad hunt along the ridges, will be lit up by the rays of the sun slowly descending into the western sea, "robing the gloom with a vesture of diverse colours, of which the threads are purple and scarlet, and the embroideries flame"; and as the light flashes from the black rocks, and the shadows deepen in the corries the superb beauty, the melancholy, the mystery of these mountains of the Isle of Mist will be revealed. But the golden glory of the sunset will melt from off the mountains, the light that silvered the great slabs will slowly fail, from out the corries darkness heralding the black night will creep with stealthy tread hiding all in gloom; and last of all, behind the darkly luminous, jagged, and fantastic outline of the Coolins the glittering stars will flash out from the clear sky, no wind will stir the great quiet, only the far-off sound, born of the rhythmic murmur of the sea waves beating on the rock-bound shore of the lonely Scavaig remains as a memory of the storm.[6]

By 1888 Collie had ascended all the main peaks of the Cuillin. In later years one of his main tasks was to measure accurately the height of every peak and pass using an aneroid barometer. This sort of measurement, which was of great help to the Ordinance Survey, established that Sgurr Alasdair and not Sgurr Dearg was the highest summit. At the end of the summer of 1888, Collie and Mackenzie made an expedition in the Cuillin which Collie in later years referred to as one of the hardest climbs of all. After an early start from Sligachan, they climbed up the Bealach na Glaic Moire to the summit of Sgurr a' Mhaidaidh. They then traversed eight of the major peaks including the Inaccessible Pinnacle by the difficult west side; made a difficult traverse around the Coire Lagan face by a route now known as Collie's ledge; made a retreat back to and over Sgurr Alasdair;

and finally as darkness was settling around them, finished the long descent of Coir' an Lochain to Loch Coruisk. They were still far from home and in the darkness they climbed 1500 feet up Druim nan Ramh on the north side of Loch Coruisk, down Harta Corrie by starlight, and along Glen Sligachan, finally arriving at the inn at midnight. This magnificent feat, not far short of the Great Traverse of the Cuillin ridge, was grand training for a man who within a few years was going to pit his strength against the mighty Himalaya.

From Skye, Collie moved out to meet the very different challenges of climbing in other parts of the British Isles. Perhaps most care and ingenuity was demanded of him by the rock faces and gullies of the English Lake District. "Climbing in the Caucasus," said A. F. Mummery, "was easy and safe; in the Alps too it was usually easy and safe, though sometimes difficult; but climbing as practised at Wasdale Head was both difficult and dangerous."[7] This was the opinion, probably expressed with tongue in cheek, of the greatest rock climber of his generation.

Wasdale Head is the traditional centre for rock climbing in the Lake District of Cumberland, Westmorland and north Lancashire. Situated in the northwest corner of England between the towns of Kendal in the south and Carlisle in the north, this countryside is renowned for the beauty of its lakes, green valleys and gentle hills. But hidden within the recesses of the hills are wonderful gullies, massive buttresses, smooth slabs and pinnacles of rock challenging enough to satisfy generation after generation of rock climbers.

The Lake District was the birthplace of British rock climbing, and in terms of the number of people climbing there, it is still the principal area in the British Isles. The area is roughly wheel-shaped in its configuration with several valleys radiating out from the hub at Scafell. From Langdale, the most accessible of the valleys from the south, the climber can easily reach Bowfell, Pavey Ark, Raven Crag, Gimmer Crag and White Ghyll: from Borrowdale, he can reach Shepherd's Crag, Thirlmere Crags, the Great Gable and Scafell. Buttermere, Wasdale Head, Eskdale, Coniston and Patterdale are all centres for Lake District ascents. The rock is mostly volcanic, either cleared tuff which gives sharp holds, or rhyolite which is dense and hard but sometimes rather smooth. The great delight for the climber in the Cumberland hills is in the gullies which are of endless variety, big or small, easy or difficult, wet or dry. The climber must be prepared to battle with mud and slime, or even fight his way upward through miniature waterfalls. But of ridges, pinnacles, cracks and slabs there are also plenty, particularly around Scafell and the Great Gable.

The Alpine Club, founded in 1854, did not in its early years consider British hills a suitable challenge. One after the other the major Alpine peaks were conquered, however, and following Edward Whymper's ascent of the Matterhorn in 1865, the feeling was prevalent that the Alps had been exploited to the limit. Between 1870 and 1890 members of the Alpine Club discovered to their intense pleasure that the British hills were worthy of more than mild scrambling at weekends. To fit in with the interests of climbers wishing to visit the Cuillin, the Lake District and Snowdonia in north Wales, a variety of clubs sprang up, many of them organized by Collie's friend William Cecil Slingsby.

Often referred to as the Father of British Mountaineering because of his enthusiasm for the sport, Slingsby was the first President of the Yorkshire Ramblers, founded in 1892, a member of the Climbers Club when it began climbing out of Pen-y-Gwryd in Snowdonia in 1898, and later Vice President of the Alpine Club. A Yorkshire squire with a passion for climbing rivalled only by Mummery himself, he had a charming personality which won him friends wherever he travelled. He was handsome, stocky, energetic, and favoured a small pointed beard. It was often said that Norway had two patron Saints—St. Olaf and Cecil Slingsby. Of Norse ancestry, he gave his greatest love to the wild peaks of Norway to which he returned time and again. In Britain he made many famous first ascents in the Lake District and Snowdonia, often climbing with Collie, his lifelong friend.

Another close friend of Collie's was Geoffrey Hastings, also a member of the three-man team that Mummery took to the Himalaya in 1895. Well-built and muscular, Hastings was renowned for his ability at step-cutting on ice. He was also a renowned campfire cook delighting in the comforts of camp life. According to Leo Amery, Hastings had a theory that it was always better to start a climb three or four hours earlier, after a comfortable sleep in a main camp, than to sleep out in discomfort in a rough bivouac on a cold mountainside. Of a quiet, retiring disposition, Hastings shunned the limelight which fell on Mummery, Slingsby and Collie. But he was every bit as able a climber, and in his first Alpine season he led a guideless ascent of the Dru, a remarkable achievement for a "beginner," even today.

Together with Mummery and Herman Woolley, who accompanied Collie on his Canadian expeditions of 1898 and 1902, these men were the founding fathers of climbing in Britain. Starting in the 1880's they climbed together for the next thirty years, not only in Britain, but in other parts

NORTHERN BRITISH ISLES SHOWING COLLIE'S CLIMBING AREAS

Hills of Sutherland

Wester Ross

Torridons

SKYE

RHUM

Cairngorms

ABERDEEN

Ben Nevis

Grampians

Glencoe

0   100
MILES

GLASGOW

ARRAN

Derryveach Mts.

SLIEVE LEAGUE   DONEGAL

BELFAST

CARLISLE

THE LAKE DISTRICT

BUTTERMERE

Pillar   Great Gable

WASDALE HEAD   Scafel

DRIGG

KENDALL

Connemara

DUBLIN

LIMERICK

Mt. Brandon

McGillicuddy's Reeks

Carrontuohill

▲ Pen Y Gwyrd

▲ Snowdown

of the world as well, setting new standards of technique, developing guideless climbing and initiating the ascent of mountains by routes of ever-increasing difficulty. They were the last of the "peak baggers" and the first of the discoverers of "new routes." Collie's position in this group was unique in that he had climbed everywhere it was possible to climb in Britain, restricting himself to no one area, although he preferred Skye to all others.

In the Lake District the pioneer climbers were Slingsby, Collie, Hastings and W. P. Haskett-Smith, who wrote *Climbing in the British Isles.* The Alpine Club had been going there for several years, but more for the scenery than for strenuous rock work in the gullies or on the rock faces. When Collie first went to Wasdale Head in 1890, he knew that there was a pinnacle of rock on Great Gable and that a good climb could be obtained on Pillar Rock. That was all. His first climb was on Napes Needle, which proved too difficult for him on that first occasion, so that he was glad of a helping hand from the first man up. He and his friends were climbing without a rope and in boots without nails, as all their equipment had been delayed at Drigg railway station. In fact they shocked Dan Tyson, proprietor of Wasdale Inn, by climbing in what he considered to be their Sunday clothes.

One Lake District climb which Collie always recalled with pleasure was that of Moss Ghyll, the most easterly of the three gullies on the great precipice of Scafell. Although several parties had ascended a considerable distance, they had all stopped underneath a huge overhanging block of rock which formed the roof of a great cave. This was the key to the whole climb, for above this obstacle there was no serious difficulty. Collie, Hastings, and a climber named Robinson gathered for the attack:

> Starting from below we chose the easiest route up the rock face on the right hand side of the ghyll. Here the climbing chiefly consisted in getting from one ledge to another, up slabs of rock. We soon, however, got into the gully itself, where we found a perpendicular wall, up which we had to climb, before reaching a ledge, which the first party of exploration had called the "Tennis Court" on account of its large size when compared with those lower down. If it were to grow vigorously, perhaps in its manhood it might just become large enough to run about on, but when we first made its acquaintance it must have been in its early childhood. From here we traversed back into the ghyll and got underneath the great overhanging block.
>
> We found that below the great slab which formed the roof another smaller one spanned the ghyll, forming the top of a great door to the

cave behind. Under this we passed, and clambered up on to the top of it. Over our heads the great rock roof stretched some distance over the ghyll. Our only chance was to traverse straight out to the right, over the side of the ghyll, till one was no longer overshadowed by the roof above, and then traverse back again above the obstacle into the ghyll once more. This was easier to plan than to carry out; absolutely no handhold could be found, but only one little projecting ledge jutting out about a quarter of an inch and about a couple of inches long to stand on; more-over, a lip of rock overhung this little ledge, making it impossible to grip it satisfactorily with one's foot. Beyond this there were six or eight feet of the nearly perpendicular rock wall to traverse.

I was asked to try it. So, being highly pleased at being intrusted with such delicate operations, I with great deliberation stretched out my foot and tried to grip the little edge with the side nails of my boot. Just as I was going to put my whole weight on to this right foot, the nails unable to hold on such a minute surface gave way, and if Hastings had not instantly with a mighty pull jerked me back, I should have been swing-ing on the rope in mid-air. But we were determined not to be beaten. Hastings' ice axe was next brought into requisition, and what followed I have no doubt will be severely criticised by more orthodox mountain-eers than myself: as it was my suggestion I must take the blame. *I hacked a step in the rock!* It was very hard work, but that upper lip to the step had to go, and Hastings' ice axe, being an extraordinary one, performed its work admirably, and without damage to anything else than the rock. I then was able to get a much firmer foothold, and getting across this bad step, clambered up the rock till I reached a spot where a capital hitch could be got over a jutting pin of rock, and the rest of the party followed. We then climbed out of the ghyll on the left up some slabs of rock.[8]

This climb provides an interesting insight into Collie's views on artificial aids to climbing. He had not the slightest doubt that the end justified the means. In a footnote to his published account of the Moss Ghyll climb, Collie defended his action: "During climbing ice and snow, one is allowed, in fact one is expected to cut steps. But it is held to be entirely contrary to the laws which govern the great sport of mountaineering to make similar holes in the rock. This is remarkable, but nevertheless true." The final outcome of this audacious act was the naming of this small excavation of rock after its sculptor. "Collie's Step" became the key to the Moss Ghyll climb for the next generation of climbers.

Collie visited all the usual places frequented by the Alpine Club in England, Scotland and Wales, but he also journeyed to more isolated spots, of which surely the most unusual for that time were the mountains

The Collie Step on the Moss Ghyll climb in the Lake District

and sea cliffs of Ireland. The mist-shrouded mountains of Ireland, although famed in legend, have until quite recently been largely ignored by mountaineers and hill-walkers. Donegal, in the far northwest of Eire, has some of the finest granite climbing in the country, with ascents of up to 1000 feet in the Derryveagh mountains. The sea cliffs along the north shore of Donegal Bay around Slieve League give good climbing. The lake district of County Galway is a beautiful part of the country, with the spectacular background of the Twelve Bens of Connemara. Further south in Kerry are the famous Macgillicuddy's Reeks, the most extensive mountainous area in the country. These mountains, which include Carrantuohill (3414 feet), the highest mountain in Ireland, give excellent rock scrambling and ridge walking. Mount Brandon (3127 feet) in the Dingle peninsula rises straight out of the sea and provides many fine climbs.

The key factors preserving these mountains from exploitation have been their remoteness and the uncertainties of Irish weather. The main railways, which run from Dublin to Galway, Limerick and Cork, end a long distance from the lonely wild regions of the northeast and southwest. In Collie's day the roads were extremely primitive, but would have provided a good training ground for the discomforts that were to follow on his Canadian journeys. The weather is too often dismissed as being simply wet and cold. In reality, although it rains in Ireland almost every day, the downpours seldom last more than half an hour.

After climbing on the sea cliffs of Slieve League on the north shore of Donegal Bay, Collie explored the sea caves to the west with some local boatmen.

> The cliffs where the cave is situated come down sheer into the dark water below; the entrance is a great doorway with a somewhat slanting roof, into which the full force of the waves from the open ocean can play; and as the boat rises and falls on the water, the danger of hidden rocks underneath the surface adds a certain amount of anxiety to the other feelings that possess one, as the daylight begins to fade away in the mysterious recesses of the cavern.[9]

The tunnel penetrated the rock for about three hundred yards before entering a large dome-shaped cavern. Off this branched several caves which they could just distinguish by the light of their candles. These caves were reputed to contain seals for which they were searching. In this gloomy region the waves surging in from the open sea produced a peculiar booming sound which echoed backwards and forwards from the rocky walls. On the voyage in, the boatmen had been describing a peculiar sea monster which inhabited the sea caves when a terrifying boom, louder than the others, reverberated down the tunnel from the open sea. Collie suggested that this must be the monster and at once the boatmen were seized with panic. Shouting to each other to row faster they raced for the daylight thus ending the attempt at cave exploration.

Although Collie explored much of Ireland, including the north coast of Mayo and around Achill Island, he felt that there were few finer hills in all the British Isles than the Twelve Bens of Connemara. This he thought all the more remarkable because they were not true mountains, the highest being only 2395 feet high. But the deep blue of the lakes, the greens and browns of the valleys and the gentle rounded hills standing out dark blue against the gathering clouds provided the most beautiful scene in all the mountainous districts of Ireland. From Connemara he travelled south to the hills of Kerry, having left them till last because they were "the most important and the highest in Ireland."

One spot in Ireland reminded Collie strongly of more northern country:

> To the west of the Macgillicuddy's Reeks, in a part of the country but little visited, is Lough Coomacullen, one of the most wonderfully beautiful mountain tarns I have seen. Hidden away amongst the hills, and difficult of access, it has attracted but little attention, yet with glacier-worn sides of bare rock that descend in many places sheer into the black waters below, and the circle of cliffs which surround the upper part of the lough, one might almost imagine one was in Norway, except that the deep velvet brown of the heather, the few well-grown hollies clinging to the broken rock walls, and the rich colours of the mosses, lichens, and ferns that find nourishment on the ledges and faces of the precipices, at once show that one is on the Atlantic coast and in a softer and warmer climate.[10]

But when he was finished with Ireland, Collie returned to the Scottish hills. Over the years he visited them all—the hills of Sutherland, Wester Ross, the Torridon group, Ben Nevis, Glencoe, Rannoch Moor, the Cairngorms, the Isle of Rhum, Arrachar and the Isle of Arran. He climbed for pleasure, to observe the marvels of nature and to see what lay behind the next range of hills, for exploration was in his blood.

In 1896, the summer after the fateful Nanga Parbat expedition, Collie returned to Skye and tackled some of the then untouched rock faces. He was joined on most of his climbs by members of the Scottish Mountaineering Club who were out in force at Sligachan. In September the Club members set about a series of new face climbs which even today are amongst the most outstanding in the Cuillin. One of Collie's favourites was the Coruisk face on Sgurr a'Greadaidh, a steep rock face almost 2000 feet high.

Other notable climbs included Sgurr Coir' an Lochain, the Basteir Tooth from Lota Corrie and Sron na Ciche. When a party led by Collie and Mackenzie made the first ascent of Sgurr Coir' an Lochain, a peak separated from the main ridge by a deep gap, the last Cuillin had capitulated. Sixty years had elapsed since Professor Forbes led the way. Am Basteir (3070 feet) is the third peak in the great Cuillin horseshoe starting from the northeast corner. Separated from it by a wide gap is the Basteir Tooth, a spectacular pinnacle of rock shaped somewhat like a decayed molar. Approached from the Lotta Corrie to the south it presents an exciting vertical climb with a mixture of cracks, chimneys, ledges and throughout a considerable sense of exposure. Collie climbed it from the gap between the Tooth and Am Basteir.

Sron na Ciche is a magnificent face of rock set at a steep angle, about 1000 feet high and two-thirds of a mile long. Situated as it is on the western side of the main Cuillin range, overlooking Glen Brittle, it was not explored by the earlier climbers who used Sligachan as their base of operations. Collie's discovery of Sron na Ciche, and the even more curious rock tower A'Chioch (the Pap), a name suggested by Mackenzie, is one of his most important contributions to the early exploration of the Cuillin. The discovery was made in 1899, when late one afternoon, Collie and Major Bruce were returning from climbing Sgurr Alisdair by the Coire Lagan on the west side. This corrie leads down from a small loch situated high on the mountainside. Collie looked across the great rock slabs of Sron na Ciche and noticed a large triangular shadow in the middle of the cliffs which was produced by the rays of the setting sun striking a curious rock tower. He photographed this unusual effect and stored it away for future reference. In 1906 when Collie was staying with his friend Colin Phillip at the Lodge in Glen Brittle, he began a systematic exploration of Sron na Ciche. The highlight of this exploration was the successful ascent of A'Chioch in company with John Mackenzie. Collie has left us the description:

> From the top of the precipice to the bottom is at least 1000 feet, perpendicular in many places and a narrow knife edge of rock about a hundred feet long runs out from it rather less than halfway down. On each side of the knife edge are steep clean slabs of rock that, at their

base, overhang the gullies below. At the end of the knife edge is placed the tower which casts its shadows across the great slab.

The climb was full of excitement for one never knew what was round the next corner. We traversed slabs, we worked up cracks and went right away from the Cioch, into the gully on the east side of it, losing sight of it altogether. Then we fortunately found a queer traverse that led out of the gully, across the perpendicular face of the cliff and back in the direction of the Cioch. But the Cioch itself we could not see until having got round several corners suddenly it came into view and we found ourselves on the end of the knife edge. We slowly made our way to the great tower at its end up which we climbed.[11]

Mackenzie led the way and was the first to step onto the famous rock tower.

By 1908 there were five routes up Sron na Ciche, three of them pioneered by Collie—the route to the summit of A'Cioch, the Western Gully and the Amphitheatre Arête. By 1923 there were eighteen routes, and by 1950 there were about twenty-eight major routes on this one rock face. But the year 1906 marked for Collie the end of the "Golden Age" of climbing in the Cuillin. After that time, although he remained active for many more years, he neither made new discoveries nor pushed through new routes. In the meantime, however, Collie had ventured into new terrain, beginning with his initiation into the Alpine world in 1892.

Chapter Three
The Alps

The Alps

The Alpine world which Collie visited in 1892 was one which was rapidly changing. All the major peaks had been climbed. The founding members of the Alpine Club were middle-aged, elderly or dead. The pioneers had been content to reach the summit by the most practical route, which had usually meant the safest and easiest, and for many years climbers had stuck to these paths. Thus the Matterhorn, the most famous of all Alpine peaks, was climbed repeatedly after 1865, but always by the two known routes—the Hörnli Ridge and the Italian Ridge. It was almost unthinkable that anyone should try the Zmutt Ridge or the Furggen Ridge, both of which had been dismissed as impractical by the Matterhorn's conqueror, Edward Whymper.

Starting about 1879, however, the new generation of climbers regarded these forbidding routes with a fresh, unbiased outlook, and decided to accept their challenge. The philosophy of climbing was changing from the simple scramble to the top, to the deliberate pitting of the climber's skill against the difficulties of the mountain. The degree of difficulty to be grappled with increased with the climber's competence, and the skills of rock climbing had increased considerably. The Alpine guides, once simple peasants accustomed to scrambling in the mountains, had become professionals, devoting themselves more and more to technique, and imparting these new skills to their clients. The younger climbers, meanwhile, were bringing to the Alps techniques learned on British mountains. This new outlook was reflected in the writings of men such as A. F. Mummery.

The true mountaineer is a wanderer, and by a wanderer I do not mean a man who expends his whole time travelling to and fro in the mountains on the exact tracks of his predecessors—much as a bicyclist rushes along the turnpike roads of England—but I mean a man who loves to be where no human being has been before, who delights in gripping rocks that have previously not felt the touch of human fingers, or in hewing his way up ice-filled gullies whose grim shadows have been sacred to the mists and avalanches since "Earth rose out of chaos." In other words, the true mountaineer is the man who attempts new ascents.[1]

The galaxy of climbing talents gathered in Chamonix in 1892 had seldom been seen together in one place in the Alps before. Included were Mummery, Hastings, Slingsby and Collie. All were first-class climbers, adventuresome, enthusiastic, fearless, blessed with vigour and vitality, and held together by the natural leadership of A. F. Mummery. Fifty years after Mummery's death, Frank Smythe, himself an outstanding mountaineer, described him as "prince among rock climbers, and the prototype of the modern rock climber and mountaineer. . . . If the old boiling-point thermometer and geological notebook excuse for mountain climbing still prevailed in certain quarters, Mummery killed it stone dead. He climbed simply and solely for the fun of the thing."[2]

Albert Frederick Mummery was born on September 10, 1855, in Dover, Kent. The son of a tanner, he was brought up in the respectable middle-class tradition of Victorian England. In early life he developed a weakness of the spine. Skinny, short-sighted, bespectacled, round-shouldered and in no way handsome, he grew up an ungainly youth who hated to be photographed. He was compensated for his physical weaknesses by an outstanding intelligence, a great sense of humour and popularity with his contemporaries, a popularity all the more remarkable because in the class-conscious Victorian era, a tanner's son who had not been to a public school was not likely to make friends in the exclusive Alpine world. As Sir Martin Conway (himself a noted mountaineer) wrote, Mummery was "unusually intelligent and gifted . . . not a mere climber. He was full of interest in interesting things. He was intellectually rather than aesthetically endowed. His mind was philosophical and at home in the abstract. Problems of political economy were especially attractive to him. He approached such questions with the same freedom from prejudice, the same original unfettered freshness of mind, with which he approached a mountain."[3]

Mummery took sufficient interest in the problems of political economy, as well as the family business, to publish a book entitled *The Physiology of Industry* in 1891. But from the time he first visited Switzerland with his family in 1871, Mummery's thoughts had never been far from the mountains. The Matterhorn had stirred his youthful imagination; he saw it

> shining in all the calm majesty of a September moon, and in the still-
> ness of an autumn night, it seemed the very embodiment of mystery
> and a fitting dwelling place for the spirits with which old legends people
> its stone swept slopes. · · 26 As I looked at it through the tangle of the
> pines or from the breezy Alps, I scarcely dared hope that one day I
> might be numbered among the glorious few who had scaled its frozen
> cliffs. Three years later the ascent had become fashionable, the deluge
> had begun, and with its earlier waves I was swept on to the long desired
> summit.[3]

Although Mummery had climbed on the chalk cliffs of Dover, contributing a chapter on the topic to Haskett-Smith's book *Climbing in the British
Isles*, and had made a few other climbs in the British Isles, he preferred
the challenge of the Alps. Between 1871 and 1879 he made a few preliminary climbs in the Alps, usually with indifferent guides, but occasionally
with Alois Burgener, the brother of Alexander Burgener, who at that time
was the most sought after guide in Chamonix. Mummery had made two
ascents of the Matterhorn and one of Mont Blanc by the regular "tourist"
routes before he was introduced to Alexander Burgener in 1879. At first
Burgener was not impressed with the debilitated, myopic young man, but
after a few preliminary test climbs, he was convinced that Mummery had
the determination and the skill to attempt some great new climb. The
project they settled on was the ascent of the Matterhorn by the Zmutt
Ridge, where two of the four faces of the splendid obelisk meet. No new
route had been tried on the Matterhorn for fourteen years. On September
3, 1879, Mummery with Burgener and two other guides, Gentinetta and
Petrus, made the first ascent of the Zmutt Ridge, beating his rival William
Penhall, who was attempting a similar route, by one and a quarter hours.
This first ascent established Mummery firmly in the forefront of Alpine
climbing and cemented his great partnership with Alexander Burgener,
which dominated the Alpine scene for the next few years.

In 1880 Mummery applied for membership in the Alpine Club, but
despite his brilliant success the previous year he was rejected. It was eight
years before he reapplied for membership. In the meantime he embarked
on new climbs with Burgener, savagely determined to succeed. In the next
two years he traversed the Col du Lion, crossed the Col du Géant, made
the first ascents of the Grands Charmoz, the Furggen Ridge of the Matterhorn, and the north and south summits of the Grépon. After his marriage
in 1883 he gave up climbing for four years, only to return in 1887 to intro-

duce his wife Mary, who was uncommonly courageous, to the Jungfrau, Dreichhorn, Rothorn, Matterhorn and the Täschhorn. In 1888 he visited the Caucasus with the guide Zurfluh, making the first ascent of Dych Tau, a peak now considered to take at least two or three days, in eleven hours. His frantic activity was finally rewarded by his election to the Alpine Club in December 1888.

When Collie made his first visit to the Alps in 1892, Mummery was not only a famous but a controversial figure. The controversy arose over his development of guideless climbing and his set views about limiting the number on a rope to two or at the most three. He had also incurred the dislike of certain respected elder members of the Alpine Club such as W. A. B. Coolidge (who could seldom agree with anyone) and Edward Whymper. It is likely that Cecil Slingsby introduced Collie into the distinguished circle of Mummery's climbing friends.

The first major climb in which Collie participated was the initial traverse of the Aiguille de Grépon. The Mont Blanc range of mountains was so dominated by the massive bulk of Mont Blanc, the highest mountain in Europe, that for many years the early climbers ignored the lesser peaks, ridges, and pinnacles which surround it. The lofty pointed summits of the granite pinnacles known as "aiguilles" appeared absolutely unassailable. The Grépon was one of these savage aiguilles. A party earlier in the season, climbing without a guide, had planted on the summit an ice axe with a fluttering scarf attached. This of course presented a challenge which Mummery was quick to take up. Supported by Hastings, Collie, and Pasteur, he determined not only to climb the Grépon, but to traverse its knife-like ridge from north to south, a feat which had not been done before. The route started from a narrow gap, the Charmoz-Grépon col, ascended the north peak, followed along the Grépon ridge to the south peak, and finally descended by the south ridge. On the south ridge was a vertical step known as the C.P. step, after the initials of an earlier climber who had painted them on the rock to mark his point of furthest progress. All parties climbing the south ridge protected their descent by fixing a rope there. Mummery therefore hired two porters to carry up ample supplies of food and drink and to fix such a rope so that the climbers could complete the traverse.

At 2 a.m. on August 18, the climbers awakened to learn that their porters, terrified of climbing the Grépon, had fled to Chamonix. With great persistence, at that early hour, Mummery rounded up a herd boy and a one-eyed guide, Gaspard Simond, who agreed to accompany them. By the dim light of candle lanterns they ascended the valley, struggled up the detestable slopes of the moraine, and as daylight was breaking struck across the Nantillon Glacier. Once onto the rocks above the glacier, Gaspard Simond's interest in the climb rapidly diminished, so he was left behind with the boy at the foot of the couloir. If the climb were unsuccessful, the party could return down the couloir to where Simond was waiting with most of the food.

Somewhat depressed by the desertion of their guide, Mummery led the remainder of the party up the couloir. When they arrived at the Charmoz-Grépon col, he had some difficulty in picking out the route up the almost vertical rock face to the north summit. At last he recognized the cleft, since known as the Mummery crack, up which his guides had led him in 1881. Of his feelings at that moment he wrote:

> Possibly the knowledge that I was going to try to lead up to it made it look worse than it really was, but for the moment I was startled at its steepness. With the exception of two steps where the rock sets back slightly (to the extent, perhaps, of two feet in all), the whole is absolutely perpendicular. In this estimate I exclude a preliminary section of seven or eight feet, which bulges out and overhangs in a most painful manner. On the other hand, it was distinctly more broken than I had expected, and the longer we looked the better we liked it, till with fair hopes of success I climbed down to the foot of the crack, scrambled onto Hastings' shoulders and tackled the toughest bit of rock climbing I have ever attempted.[4]

For the first person climbing up the crack, the rope offered no protection beyond the first twenty feet where a hitch around a great splinter provided some security against an unexpected fall. About halfway up there was a narrow, sloping hold for the feet, but beyond this the difficulties increased. With few holds for his hands, and almost none for his feet, Mummery relied on a few loose stones wedged in the crack to provide a wobbling support for his upward progress. The climbers below watched in deathly silence until after an interminable time Mummery's head and arms disappeared over the top of the slab of rock which abuts against the crack. Once secured above the crack, he ordered his companions to come up while he protected them with the rope. Then they scrambled up a short gully, through a hole in the ridge called the "Kanones Loch," and up to the north peak. Beyond this was a great gap in the ridge, which the party descended one by one on a hundred feet of rope. Mummery was the last down on the rope, and at one point he paused to rest on a small knob of rock. To

The Grépon in the Alps. The line between the two "X's" marks Mummery's crack

Mummery climbing Mummery's crack. Photograph taken on climb with Collie, Hastings and Slingsby'

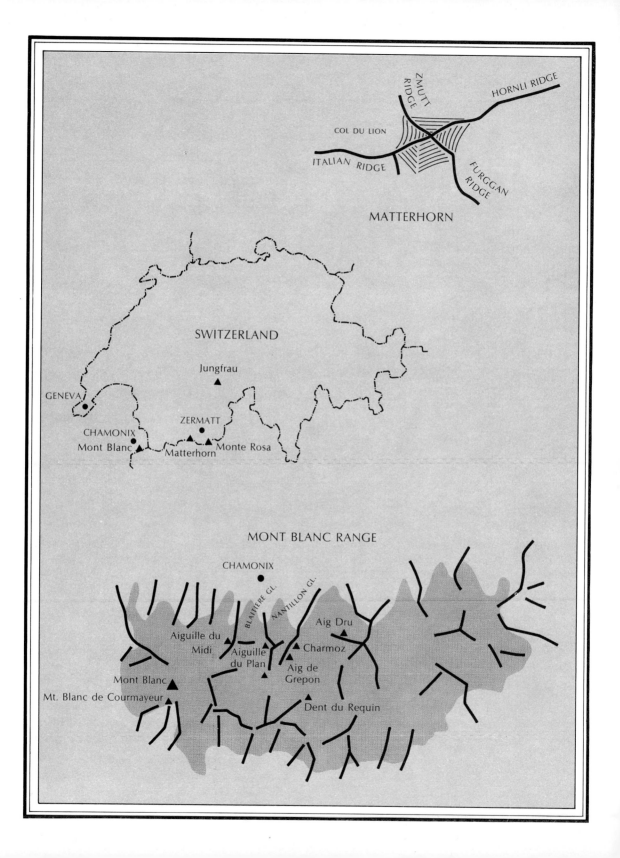

his horror the rope on which they had all been relying came loose from its fixture above. Only by the use of his superb reflexes and strength was Mummery able to cling to the rock, and then, directed by Collie, to complete a seemingly impossible descent without the aid of the rope. His reputation of being "like a spider on steep rocks" was well deserved.

The party advanced towards the South Peak, a formidable enough objective which they proposed to climb by throwing a rope over the top. Collie had already picked up two stones suitable for weighting the rope and was preparing to throw it, when Pasteur found a fairly easy crack which not only led to the summit but linked up with the C.P. route. Within a few minutes they scrambled to the top of the ridge and in the howling wind crowded around the ice axe with its fluttering flag. It was too cold to remain on the summit, so they scrambled down into the lee of the ridge to a celebration lunch and Bouvier*. The descent was not without its funny side. Roping down from a piton, Hastings was unlucky enough to jam his foot in a crack. On the advice of his friends, he finally unlaced the boot, pulled his foot out, and then retrieved the boot. This was an amusing performance for everyone except the unhappy Hastings, who was suspended on a perpendicular rock face by a rope dangling from a piton of doubtful security. At the C.P. gap the porters were on hand to help them up the lowered rope and at a safe resting place they consumed the remaining food and brandy. Full of good cheer they raced down the route which they had ascended so laboriously early in the morning, arriving back at the hotel at 5 p.m. to be welcomed by kind friends and a vast pot of tea.

The next year, after only one season in the Alps, Collie was elected to the Alpine Club on his first application. This was in recognition not only of a highly successful season the previous year, but of his considerable contribution to the advancement of mountaineering in Great Britain. July 1893 once again found Collie at Chamonix with Slingsby, Hastings and Mummery. Collie made several important climbs including the first ascent of the Dent du Requin, the Petit Dru, and the Matterhorn by the Italian Ridge. Perhaps the outstanding climb was the first ascent of the Aiguille du Plan by the west face. It was certainly an audacious feat, for only twelve months previously Mummery and Slingsby had been beaten back exhausted and hungry after spending two days struggling up its icy cliffs.

On the morning of August 6, 1893, two porters were sent ahead to carry tents, sleeping bags and supplies to the extreme left moraine of the Blaitière Glacier. Here in the shade of the pines, a festive lunch was

---

*A fortified French wine.

prepared with Mummery spilling the soup, Hastings frying the bacon, and Collie producing a pot of refreshing tea. Then they headed up the glacier carrying great bundles of sticks for firewood. Collie and Hastings set about erecting the camp in a sheltered grassy hollow while Mummery and Slingsby explored the route ahead. The latter on their return found that Collie had unearthed a ruined chalet, which, skillfully roofed with the groundsheet, had been converted into a crude shelter for the night. "Slingsby and I, with our usual magnanimity, expressed our willingness to put up with the inferior accommodation of the tent," Mummery reported. "From various remarks at breakfast the next morning—or ought I to say the same night?—I inferred that our generosity had not been without its reward."[5]

The climb commenced at 1:45 a.m. under a cloudless sky, with the stars shining brightly. Led by Collie and Slingsby, they followed up an old moraine to reach the glacier above a minor icefall. Slowly they worked their way up the glacier, which steadily steepened as it rose to an ice-coated couloir. After a short pause for a second breakfast at 5:25 a.m., they scrambled up the rocks at the side of the couloir until finally the absence of any holds forced them into the couloir. It was a difficult, dangerous place, as down its centre ran a deep trough made by falling stones, ice and water. All efforts to escape by climbing onto the rocks to the right were defeated. About 250 feet higher up they escaped into a gully, from whence they climbed over broken rock to a slab twelve feet high with only one small knob of rock, almost out of reach, for a handhold. Despite his agility, Mummery had to make three attempts before climbing this slab, which brought them onto easier rocks. At another point higher up they made a traverse back over some dangerous slabs into the couloir, their progress safeguarded by running the rope through a piton. The ascent of the couloir again proved difficult because of the danger of falling rock, and the possibility that chunks of ice dislodged by the axe would fall on the unprotected heads of the climbers further down. To avoid these dangers, Mummery brought the whole party up to his level before cutting across the shining ice of the couloir to firm rock on the right. There then followed some hair-raising gymnastics as the climbers followed Mummery up vertical slabs, over bulging rocks, up thin cracks and along slender ledges.

Finally they were forced into a steep gully where upward progress was prevented by a number of great plate-like stones jammed together and forming a roof-like structure over their heads. Here they halted to consume a snack of ginger, biscuits, and chocolate which Hastings, with his usual aplomb, produced from his capacious pockets. Then Mummery turned his attention to the overhanging rocks: "This difficulty appeared worse in prospect than in actual fact it proved to be, and beyond the mental discomfort induced by hanging on to doubtfully secure stones, and climbing outwards over a very high cliff in a semi-horizontal position—much indeed as a fly walks along a ceiling—the obstruction was passed without difficulty."[6] Above them the way to the col was obvious along a short steep slope of ice. The view was dramatic. Behind them was the overhanging cliff up which they had climbed. To the north the col was shut in by a huge pinnacle of smooth precipitous slabs recalling the relentless cruelty of the great precipice on the Little Dru; and to the south great ice cliffs overhung a vast rugged wall of rock. It was up this great wall that they began to climb shortly after noon.

Halfway up a massive overhanging cornice of ice and snow had to be overcome. This was effected with great difficulty by hoisting Mummery onto a living pyramid of Hastings and Slingsby, while Collie protected them with a rope. One by one they scrambled onto each other's shoulders and over the obstacle until finally, Collie, who was last on the rope, was left below with no helping shoulder to climb onto.

> Unfortunately we were so far up the slope, and the projecting lip so deflected and cut off all sound, that we could not hear what Collie said. All we could do was to haul with one accord, but we soon found our efforts ceased to have any effect, . . . Collie, however, proved equal to the emergency; finding that his head and shoulders refused to go over the lip, he stuck his feet against the ice and, forcing himself outwards against the rope, walked up the overhanging ice in a more or less horizontal position. This manoeuvre brought him, feet uppermost, onto the slope, and it is needless to say caused astonishment and mirth to the spectators. However, he soon resumed a more normal attitude and tracked up the slope to a little crevasse.[7]

From this point Mummery cut steps in the ice slope, and a hundred feet higher reached the main ridge. A huge cornice on the ridge overhung the tremendous cliffs above the little Glacier d'Envers Blatière. Well to the right of the cornice the route led up to the final tower, which had been climbed by the southwestern ridge when the first ascent was made. A few steep gullies and crags led Mummery and his party to the summit at 2 p.m. Here in glorious sunshine they basked on the warm rocks for an hour and a half, before reluctantly setting off down the steep snow slope leading to the Glacier du Requin. After a few minor adventures they arrived back at the hotel at 9 p.m., nineteen hours after the start of the climb. The proprietor of the hotel immediately provided a substantial dinner to which all their friends were invited. The convivial party continued well into the next morning, so that early breakfasters were astonished to find dinner still in progress. This kind of merry-making was very much a part of Mummery's Alpine activity where everything had a wonderful zest to it. One wonders if the same kind of jollity was permitted in English and Scottish inns of those days.

In 1894 the group of climbers was reduced to Mummery, Collie and Hastings, who very likely then finalized their plans to climb in the Himalaya the next summer, a trip which Mummery had been considering since 1891. Certainly their high calibre of climbing continued, and during the month of August they performed a first and guideless ascent of Mont Blanc by the Brenva face. This climb began with an ascent to a bivouac high on the Brenva Glacier where, on a perfect August evening, they watched the sun go down. The next day Mummery led them in a fierce struggle up the steep icy slopes. Every step had to be cut with the ice axe and they missed the presence of guides who excelled at step cutting. This delayed them so that by nightfall they were 1500 feet below the summit. The second night was spent perched on a rock thousands of feet above the Brenva Glacier. The intense cold added to the misery of hunger kept them awake most of the night. On the morning of the third day they were unable to move until the sun's rays warmed them. The climb continued relentlessly up the steep ice until late in the afternoon they cut through the overhanging edge of the Mont Blanc snowcap. Collie recalled that he arrived on the summit by crawling on his hands and knees. This climb was an example of Mummery's lack of foresight, his tendency to underestimate difficulties and his failure to provide food and warm clothing for a second night out. These mistakes were repeated in the Himalaya.

During the same month they made a first ascent of the Col des Courtes, the Aiguille Verte by the Main Ridge, and the third ascent of the Matterhorn by the Zmutt Ridge. This last climb was carried out in company with the Duke of the Abruzzi, who thereafter decided to devote his time and money to mountain exploration. He became famous by climbing Mount St. Elias in Alaska in 1897 and the peaks of the Ruwenzori (Mountains of the Moon) in 1906, and attempting K2 in 1909. On the Zmutt Ridge, Mummery followed slightly to the right of his old route of 1879. Because of the absence of snow and ice, they were able to climb short distances on the very exposed north and west faces of the Matterhorn, thus avoiding overhanging parts of the ridge. They reached the summit by 10 a.m., which speaks well of their skill and the excellence of their training.

Collie climbing in the Alps c. 1893

Collie returned to the Alps in 1899 with Major C. G. Bruce, whom he had met in India, and his Ghurka orderly, and in 1905 he visited the Italian Alps with Woolley. But his fondest memories were of the glorious days he spent with Mummery. In later years he wrote:

> There are few more pleasurable sensations than to be comfortable and warm under the lee of some boulder, watching the stars as they slowly move westward; or to sit by a camp fire after the sun has set, and to recall all the enjoyment of the climb just finished; a feeling of most profound contentment with everything in the world steals over the party; the conversation becomes more disjointed as first one then another turns over and sleeps.
>
> When I look back and think of all the various places where Mummery, Hastings, Slingsby, and I have slept out in the open, far away from the haunts of men, and remember how we enjoyed ourselves, I for one would go back year after year to the Alps if those times could be brought back again. In those days the glass of time, when shaken, ran in golden sands. Now all that is left of them is the memory.[8]

Although Hastings was to accompany Collie to Canada and Collie to join Slingsby in his "northern playground," Mummery was to be one of the party only one last time, for the awesome task of testing a Himalayan giant.

Chapter Four
Nanga Parbat I

Nanga Parbat I

5, Castlemount Terrace,
Dover.

Dear Collie,

Praise God and get your luggage ready. Viceroy telegraphs to Godley, "Please communicate the following to Mummery, your proposal is accepted." I wired you this morning and hope you got it alright.

I shall write Bruce tomorrow asking him to engage a good cook and a man who can speak English and the native lingo. Also baggage ponies.

Yours in haste.
A.F. Mummery

P.S. Can you get me two of the Shetland vests like you had last year? I think they would make good garments for Nanga, light and warm. Come down when you get a chance.

With the receipt of official approval announced in this letter to Collie, Mummery's dreams of climbing in the Himalaya were finally to be realized in 1895. According to Sir Martin Conway, he, D. W. Freshfield, and Mummery had agreed in April 1891 to meet in Darjeeling in September to climb Kanchenjunga. When Freshfield dropped out shortly afterwards, the other two postponed the date and changed the climb to K2. They were to meet for preliminary climbs in the Alps during the summer, but it soon became evident to Conway that Mummery was not interested in the kind of expedition he proposed to make. Conway wanted to explore the whole district, to take an artist with him and prepare sketches, drawings and maps. In addition he wanted to make a scientific collection of the flora and fauna and geology of the region. These matters were of little interest to Mummery, who wanted to find the biggest mountains and spend all the energies of the expedition in climbing them. For these reasons Mummery and Conway decided to part company.

As leader of his own expedition, Mummery had settled on climbing Nanga Parbat, at 26,600 feet the sixth highest mountain in the world. It is exceeded only by Everest, Godwin-Austen (K2), Kanchenjunga, Makalu and Dhaulagiri. These peaks have now all been climbed, but only after years of exploration, and the unsuccessful attempts of many expeditions. These expeditions, consisting of many climbers, were usually supported by trained Sherpas, high altitude porters, oxygen equipment, tons of supplies and scientific expertise gained often under harsh conditions on the mountains. Between 1921 and 1953, for example, eleven major expeditions travelled to Everest, eight of them with the express purpose of climbing to the top. Prior to the successful climb of Hillary and Tenzing on May 29, 1953, only five Europeans and one Sherpa had climbed to within 1000 feet of the summit, and a number of lives had been lost. Since 1953, a memorable day in the annals of mountaineering, all the major summits in the world have been climbed. Furthermore the science of high altitude climbing has advanced to such an extent that small climbing parties are now pioneering new and more difficult routes up the giants of the Himalaya.

Nanga Parbat achieved a fearsome reputation among the great peaks. Prior to its conquest by Hermann Buhl on July 3, 1953, fourteen European climbers and seventeen porters had died attempting to reach its summit. The worst disaster on the mountain occurred on the night of June 14, 1937, when an avalanche overwhelmed seven climbers and nine porters at Camp IV, high on the mountain. Only one climber survived, a German who was at base camp at the time of the disaster.

A more bizarre tragedy than this had occurred in 1934. On this expedition, three climbers supported by eleven porters pitched their tents at Camp VIII, at a point estimated to be 900 feet below the summit. The party was beset by a violent storm, and on July 8, after two days and nights without sleep, they decided to retreat. In the ensuing débacle, six porters and two German climbers died on the descent to lower camps. On July 13, the storm cleared, and the other members of the expedition at lower camps saw three men slowly climbing down from Camp VII. The next day one of the three, the orderly Angstering, staggered into Camp IV in the last stages of exhaustion, with the news that Willy Merkl, the "Leader of the Nanga Parbat Expedition" whom Collie had once declined to speak with, and his orderly Gay-Lay were somewhere on the mountain between

Camps VII and VI. Their cries could be heard by the watchers below, who were helpless to move up the mountain in their exhausted condition. The last cries from Willy Merkl were heard on July 15, seven days after the storm struck. It was presumed that Merkl and Gay-Lay had died where they had been left by Angstering, but in 1938 Merkl's friend Fritz Bechtold stood once more on the east arête and discovered that Merkl must have dragged himself up to a rocky prominence known as the Moor's Head. The bodies of Merkl and Gay-Lay, perfectly preserved after four years on the mountain, were buried where they were found. The only equipment they had with them was one blanket and a piece of foam rubber.

It was this peak, with a reputation until then unspoiled by disaster, that Mummery, Hastings and Collie planned to climb during the summer of 1895. They had applied to the Indian Government in 1894 for permission to travel through Kashmir and visit the eastern Himalayas. The Government provided additional help through the services of Major C. G. Bruce, an army officer interested in exploration climbing and the use of Ghurka soldiers for high altitude portering. The liason with Major Bruce, who had accompanied Sir Martin Conway, was of great help to the expedition. With the minimum of preparation the three climbers arranged to set off in June and return sometime in September, later than the usual end of the European climbing season. Collie was given special leave of absence by his chief, Professor Ramsay of University College, London, a reflection of the more leisurely pace at which life was lived in the nineteenth century.

To the formidable task these three men brought only their splendid skills as mountaineers. Mummery had the advantage of having climbed Dych Tau (17,054 feet high), in the Caucasus, whereas Hastings and Collie had climbed no higher than Mont Blanc (15,781 feet). Mummery's experience had been misleading, however, as he had climbed Dych Tau in a little over eleven hours. Russian climbers even today regard this peak as quite formidable, and allow at least two days for its ascent. Mummery had chosen his companions well; they were accustomed to climbing together in the Alps, and had been tested by the severest difficulties. Furthermore, they had for several years accustomed themselves to climbing without guides and to making their own routes up the mountain face. In coming to the Himalaya without Swiss guides, they were setting a new precedent.

Their decision to seek new fields for exploration was partly influenced by a feeling of overcrowding and lack of solitude in the Alps. In Collie's opinion, the Alps were "as dead as Queen Anne—they have been overwhelmed in the waters of oblivion!" In addition to the prevalent opinion that no climber should ascend the same peak twice, there was the much stronger feeling that greater glory lay in reaching the summit of a peak previously untouched by man. Mummery and Collie were too fond of the mountains to pay much attention to the first opinion, but they would have been less than human to ignore the second. Collie wrote that "as access to the Alps and other snow ranges becomes easier and easier year by year, the mountaineer, should he wish to test his powers against the unclimbed hills, must perforce go further afield."[1] In 1895 all the European peaks had long since been climbed, and the next phase of the sport, the ascent by different and more difficult routes, was only in its infancy. It was therefore quite natural to seek fresh conquests overseas, but it was a measure of Mummery's vigorous enthusiasm, fearlessness and strong ambition that he chose a Himalayan giant for his next attempt.

The choice of Nanga Parbat was ambitious by any standards both at the time and later. In 1895 the distance of India from England, the natural difficulties of the country, the lack of provisions, the almost total absence of roads, and the disturbed political conditions made the task of reaching the mountain appear almost more impossible than the ascent itself. In theory the British held the two thousand mile southern slope of the Himalaya. Tibet on the northern slopes was almost unexplored and remained closed to Europeans until Sir Francis Younghusband, the first European to cross the Gobi Desert, penetrated to Lhasa with a military mission in 1904. Nepal and Bhutan on the southern slopes were closed to all foreigners, and only the tiny state of Sikkim, about thirty miles wide, offered safe travel for Europeans to the foot of the great peaks.

The western Himalaya, because of the greater distance from the sea, was a more arid and less attractive region than the eastern Himalaya around Everest. Nevertheless, for political reasons the western ranges were more accessible. The fertile valley of the Indus, the mighty river of Pakistan which arises to the north of Nanga Parbat and enters the sea near Karachi, had long been protected by British forces against the marauding tribesmen of Baluchistan, Afghanistan and the Hindu Kush. Russia, the greatest potential threat to the British in India, pressed closest on the frontier about one hundred miles north of Nanga Parbat. In a series of diplomatic moves and border skirmishes the British Government in India had ensured the peaceful settlement of the border states at the western end of the Himalaya. Kashmir in 1895 was a prosperous country; the partial pacification of Chitral had been achieved after a hard-fought campaign which was witnessed by the young Winston Churchill; and at that time a military road had just been pushed through from Kashmir to Gilgit. This road travelled round the eastern flank of the Nanga Parbat range and simplified the approach to that mountain. The natives around Nanga Parbat were friendly, although the Chilas tribesmen who lived on the western slopes were unpredictable. The Hunzas who lived to the north around Baltit were to prove in the years to come almost as skilled mountaineers as the renowned Sherpas of Nepal.

The earliest recorded mountaineer in the Himalaya was a Captain Gerard who in 1818 attempted the ascent of Leo Porgyul in the Spiti district, but was unsuccessful after reaching a height of 19,400 feet. Ten years later he made the first successful ascent of an unnamed mountain of 20,400 feet. From 1848 to 1850, Sir Joseph Hooker, the famous botanist, travelled from Darjeeling into Sikkim and eastern Nepal. The first explorers with previous Alpine mountaineering experience were two brothers, Adolph and Robert Schlagintweit, who travelled through a large portion of the Himalaya from 1854 to 1858. They made an unsuccessful attempt on Kamet (25,443 feet), remaining on its slopes for two weeks with a highest camp at around 19,000 feet. They were forced to turn back after reaching a highest estimated altitude of 22,259 feet. On the return journey, after exploring the upper valley of the Indus north of Kashmir, Adolph Schlagintweit was murdered at Kashgar.

Englishmen and Indians employed by the British Trigonometrical Survey carried out the first systematic exploration in the Himalaya. Disguised as Nepalese herdsmen, Buddhist pilgrims and Tibetan merchants, a number of adventurers penetrated the frontiers of these forbidden lands. Many disappeared; a few returned with surreptitious maps and measurements; still fewer travelled beyond the more civilized towns to reach small communities in the high foothills where herdsmen were willing to aid them in climbing the lower peaks.

From 1860 to 1865 W. H. Johnson, an enthusiastic mountaineer, was engaged on the Kashmir Survey. He established a large number of trigonometrical stations at heights of over 20,000 feet. In 1865 he ascended two peaks which measured around 22,000 feet. Other officers on the Kashmir Survey were Captain T. G. Montgomerie, who in 1856 had discovered K2, the second highest Himalayan peak, and H. H. Godwin-Austen, who explored and surveyed it. They explored the Astor, Gilgit and Skardu districts, and must therefore have been the first to survey Nanga Parbat. Godwin-Austen also explored the Baltoro Glacier, a remarkable achievement when the use of ice axes and ropes even in the Alps was very limited.

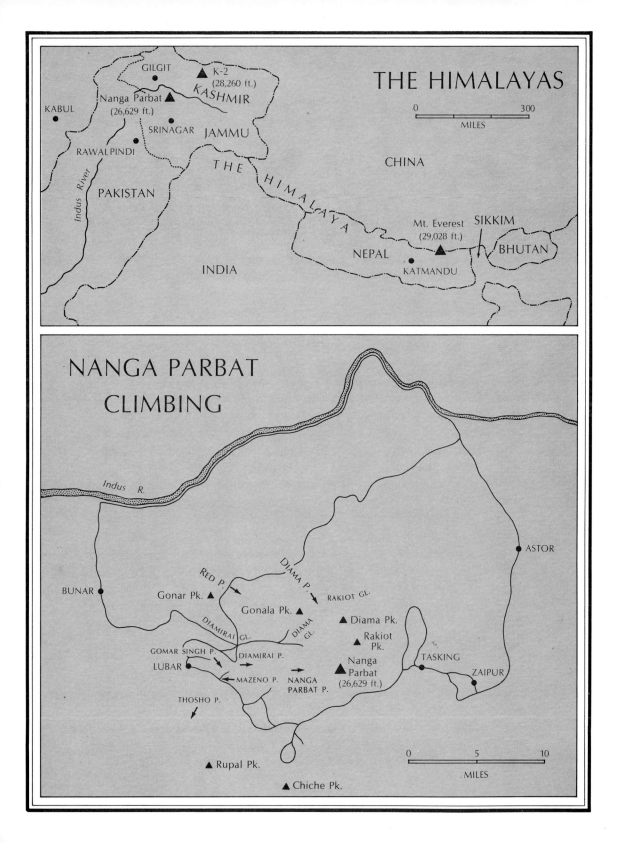

THE HIMALAYAS

GILGIT

▲ K-2
(28,260 ft.)

KASHMIR

Nanga Parbat
(26,629 ft.) ▲

KABUL

SRINAGAR

JAMMU

RAWALPINDI

THE

HIMALAYA

CHINA

0   300
MILES

Mt. Everest
(29,028 ft.)

SIKKIM

Indus River

PAKISTAN

NEPAL

BHUTAN

INDIA

KATMANDU

NANGA PARBAT
CLIMBING

Indus R.

ASTOR

BUNAR

RED P.

DIAMA P.

Gonar Pk. ▲

RAKIOT GL.

Gonala Pk. ▲

▲ Diama Pk.

DIAMIRAI GL.

DIAMA GL.

▲ Rakiot
Pk.

GOMAR SINGH P.

DIAMIRAI P.

LUBAR

TASKING

Nanga
Parbat
(26,629 ft.) ▲

ZAIPUR

MAZENO P.

NANGA
PARBAT P.

THOSHO P.

0   5   10
MILES

▲ Rupal Pk.

▲ Chiche Pk.

The highest summit to be reached for almost fifty years fell in 1883, when W. W. Graham came to India with Swiss guides. This was the first serious attempt at mountaineering in the Himalaya by trained climbers since the expedition of the Schlagintweit brothers some thirty years earlier. Their highest ascent was Mount Kabru (24,015 feet) in Sikkim, lying to the southwest of Kanchenjunga. Sir Martin Conway's party in 1892 explored a large part of the Mustagh range lying northeast of Nanga Parbat, including many passes in that region, and made the first ascent of the Baltoro Glacier since Godwin-Austen, twenty years before. They ascended Crystal Peak (19,400 feet), near the head of the Baltoro Glacier, and obtained a spectacular view of the Mustagh Tower. A few days later they caught a view of K2. Major Bruce, accompanied by Captain Young-husband, continued climbing in the neighbourhood of Chitral, to the northwest of Nanga Parbat, the following year.

When Mummery and his party set out, information concerning mountaineering in the Himalaya was very limited. Although available maps were imperfect, Kashmir and the Karakoram range had been fairly accurately surveyed in the 1860's. The two expeditions to the Baltoro Glacier had passed close to Nanga Parbat, which lay on the direct route to Gilgit. Nanga Parbat was accessible; K2 and the Mustagh Tower were not. The reason for Mummery's choice, apart from the accessibility of the mountain, may have been influenced by two other factors: the appointment of Major Bruce as liaison officer, and the possible spread of information among the Swiss guides by their brethren who had already been to the Himalaya. Although Mummery at this time was performing guideless climbs, he would still be attuned to the latest reports in Grindelwald of anything new in the climbing world. Graham's account of his 1883 Himalayan Expedition in the *Alpine Journal* would have certainly aroused much interest.

In reflecting on Mummery's three-man expedition it is almost incredible to see how light-heartedly and with what stupendous faith in their own ability they advanced on their terrible objective. The notion that climbing a Himalayan peak was very much different from climbing Mont Blanc had not yet been propounded. There is no record that Mummery, Collie or Hastings had ever suffered from altitude sickness prior to 1895, although the malady had been described by others. The greatest difficulty to be overcome at high altitude is the lack of oxygen. A dweller at sea level may eventually become accustomed to working at 14,000 feet, but even Sherpas who spend all their lives at high altitudes become dulled and weakened above 18,000 feet. Above 21,000 feet a progressive deterioration of physique takes place, leading to a rapid loss of weight and appetite, to sleeplessness and a great reduction of physical and nervous energy. Headaches, hallucinations, loss of judgement, pneumonia, pulmonary edema, collapse and death may all result from even short exposure to high altitude. Collie was familiar with the reduction of the barometric pressure at high altitudes from his use of a variety of altimeters. Both Mummery and Collie were aware that at a high altitude the air became much "thinner," but relevant information on reduced pressure of oxygen at high altitudes was not worked out until 1911. In that year John S. Haldane, a physiologist originally interested in deep sea diving, turned his attention to the problems of high altitude on Colorado's Pike's Peak (14,110 feet). Collie, however, knew of Sir Joseph Hooker's account of the headaches, giddiness and lassitude he had suffered while crossing a snow pass of 16,000 feet in 1849, and as a scientist, must surely have known of other examples occurring amongst climbers in the Alps.

In Himalayan expeditions a second major problem, and one over which there is limited control, is the weather. Mummery's expedition gave no serious thought to the possibility of a prolonged spell of bad weather. The monsoon, bringing clouds, gales and snowstorms, usually reaches the western Himalaya by the first week in July. The successful ascent of Nanga Parbat was made on July 3, 1953, in a year when the monsoon broke on July 14. As a rule climbing must be suspended during the monsoon; although there may be occasional clear spells of a few days' duration, the heavy snowfall on the mountainside makes all movement up and down extremely difficult. The onset of the monsoon on July 8, 1934, resulted in the tragic deaths described earlier in this chapter. Mummery, entirely ignorant of these meteorological possibilities, began serious climbing on July 18, and all climbing ceased on September 16. They had incredibly good luck with the weather during this time, although Collie mentions that winter had set in by the middle of September, when the snow on the Diamirai Glacier made climbing impossible. Such good luck with the weather was not accorded any subsequent expedition.

The question of the equipment used by Mummery's expedition is of considerable interest. Their clothing was of the ordinary outdoor type worn by English sportsmen of that day. It is more than likely that collar and tie were worn, just as in climbing in Switzerland or in the Canadian Rockies at that time. The only concession to the penetrating cold of high altitude was an extra woolen sweater, such as the Shetland vests

Base camp in the Rupal Valley, Nanga Parbat, July 1895. Bruce is standing, Mummery sitting

Mummery asked for in his letter to Collie. Their boots were metal studded, and of the type ordinarily used in the Alps. Their unfortunate porters were not provided with boots or special clothes other than the few rags they customarily wore. Mummery had brought the small "Mummery" tent made of silk and weighing only three and a half pounds. This tent could be supported by two ice axes, thus reducing the weight to be carried; but having no insulation, it was scant protection against the cold. The party had ice axes and ropes, perhaps the light ropes of high quality developed by Mummery, but no crampons, so essential for safe climbing on ice. For fuel they relied mainly on wood carried by porters, but they had one small spirit cooking stove.

Lack of food was a constant source of anxiety. They intended relying on local supplies of flour, chickens and goats, but these were only obtainable if one of the Europeans descended to the valley to engage in prolonged barter with the tribesmen. The flour was coarse, being mixed with stone dust from the primitive grindstones. The abrasive effect of this mixture had a harmful effect on their digestion. The supplies of food and drink brought with them from Kashmir were all used up within a month, and there were long delays in the arrival of the fresh supplies they had ordered to be sent up to the mountain. The Kashmir merchants were willing to supply anything from Bass's beer to Huntley and Palmer's biscuits, from tinned meat to English flour. But once a deposit had been paid they were slow to deliver.

The modern Himalayan climber might envy Mummery his lack of concern over the commissariat arrangements but could scarcely suppress an "I told you so" when these arrangements broke down. However, the modern climber would certainly envy the speed with which the 1895 travellers passed through customs. They left England on June 20 and arrived in Bombay on July 5. That night they boarded the train, and two days later arrived in Rawalpindi. In seventeen days they had crossed four frontiers, but there were none of the exasperating delays due to lost baggage or customs restrictions which are the curse of modern expeditions.

At Rawalpindi, twelve miles from Islamabad, the modern capital of Pakistan, they could see for the first time the foothills of the Himalaya rising out of the plains of the Punjab. Here they were poised on the threshold of the greatest single adventure that any one of them would ever undertake. In a letter to his wife dated July 10, 1895, Mummery described the excitement of their journey. From Rawalpindi they followed a well travelled road to the town of Baramula in the Vale of Kashmir. They met many English people en route. They were conveyed in tongas, small two-wheeled carriages with light springs. The horses, which galloped at high speed were changed every few miles. The monsoon broke during the journey and the torrential rain washed out parts of the road and one bridge. This caused little delay as the government provided numerous coolies to haul the tongas over the rough patches. At Baramula they met for the first time, Major Bruce, who had travelled 120 miles from Abbottabad to hire ponies, supplies, coolies and a cook for them. After making these arrangements Bruce had to return to his regiment leaving them to proceed on their own. "Everyone is going far out of his way to help us," concluded Mummery, "and as for climbing difficulties, there are no serious ones to encounter, and though the rarity of the air may bother us, it can't hurt us in any way. I rather expect we shall do about three weeks walking and exploring after we get to Astor, as we may fairly expect better weather but not so good as I expect to have it for Nanga [Parbat]."[2]

Collie shared Mummery's enthusiasm for the beauty of the Vale of Kashmir. He described it as a "land of lakes and waterways, splendid trees and old ruins, vines, grasslands, flowers and pine forests watered by cool streams from the snow ranges that encircle it, with a climate during the summer months like that of the south of France—no wonder this valley of Kashmir is beautiful." Unlike Mummery Collie did not express any rash opinion about the absence of any climbing difficulties ahead, but he was writing after the event, whereas Mummery was describing the events as they occurred, and at the same time hastening to reassure his wife.

On July 11, having crossed the Woolar Lake, they loaded the ponies and crossed the Raj Diangam Pass (11,950 feet), to the village of Curais, where arrangements were made to obtain fresh ponies. The next morning the village chief used every kind of lie, with the utmost oriental politeness, to assure them that no ponies were available. Mummery immediately wrote out a telegram addressed to the British Resident at Srinagar, asking what should be done to the miserable official at Curais who refused the British party help and ponies. The telegram was translated to the unfortunate chieftain, who in ten minutes produced three times as many ponies as could be used.

On July 14, the party crossed the Kamri Pass and from its summit obtained the first view of Nanga Parbat, over forty miles away. Collie described it as "rising in dazzling whiteness far above all the intervening ranges. There is nothing in the Alps that can at all compare with it in grandeur, and although often one is unable to tell whether a mountain is really big, or only appears so, this was not the case with Nanga Parbat as seen from the Kamri. It was huge, immense; and instinctively we took off our hats in order to show that we approached in a proper spirit."[3]

Camping at Rattu on July 15, they met Lieutenant C. G. Stewart, who was camped there with his mountain battery. He showed them the guns, weighing two hundred and twenty-four pounds each, which he had taken over the Shandur Pass in deep snow to the relief of the fort at Chitral. The forcing of the Shandur Pass, described later by Winston Churchill, was one of the most desperate pieces of work in the relief of Chitral, as the enemy were under the impression that even troops without mountain guns could not cross the pass in winter. After an entertaining evening with Stewart, who regaled them with tales of this hard-fought campaign, the party moved on the next day.

When they arrived at the village of Zaipur on the southeast corner of the Nanga Parbat range, they were anxious to cross over the raging Rupal torrent, but there was no ford or bridge. The villagers, however, were most willing to help, and aided by the men from Chorit, a village on the further side, about sixty men began building a makeshift bridge. Tons of stones and brushwood were built out into the raging torrent. Next pine trees were neatly fixed on a cantilever principle, and finally several thick trunks about fifty feet long were toppled across and lashed in place with Alpine rope. After three hours of hard work the bridge was finished. The reward for this magnificent achievement was two rupees each for the headmen of the two villages. How this was divided among the sixty followers was not recorded. Crossing the bridge, the party passed through the small villages of Chorit and Tashing, and twenty-seven days after leaving London, established a base camp.

The next day, July 17, the climbers relaxed while the servants organized the camp. Mummery seized the opportunity to write another letter to his wife:

> We have just got to the foot of our peak. The journey has been long, but very luxurious, and we have had all our tents and luggage carried up here. With porters at fourpence a day it is not necessary to limit one's luggage. Our cook is a brilliant success, and feeds us in great splendour. Our other men are today occupied in washing our clothes, though I doubt if the results will be all that can be desired.
>
> Our first business will be to get into condition. I expect we shall start for an 18,000 or 19,000 feet peak tomorrow: there are plenty about here, but mostly snow grinds. However, that is good for the wind. I don't

think there will be any serious mountaineering difficulties on Nanga, and the peak is much freer from hanging glaciers than I had expected. I fancy the ascent will be mainly a question of endurance. We are in excellent spirits, but our legs don't work as well as they should, so we shall devote three weeks to having walks.

You may expect to get a wire about August 17, or a few days later. Our expedition has been notified to all local authorities, and instructions given to help us in any way we want. You can, therefore, picture us well provided and taken care of. . . . Don't be anxious about us. We shall not get into any difficulties. [4]

Unfortunately, the sequel did not bear him out.

The camp was situated on the north bank of the Rupal River a few miles west of the village of Tashing. The accompanying map illustrates the direction of their travels over the next few weeks. The Rupal Valley runs westward from the Thosho Pass, under the whole stupendous southern face of Nanga Parbat, till it joins the valley coming down from the Kamri Pass, some eight miles beyond Tashing. The Valley is about twenty-five miles long in a straight line, but half of it is filled with the Rupal Glacier, and the travellers were confronted with interminable ups and downs, twists and turns. The terrain they crossed varied from icy crevassed glacier, to steep moraine, to loose rocks and debris. At times the raging side torrents sweeping down from the melting snows of Nanga Parbat had to be crossed, always a dangerous and uncomfortable performance. The Nanga Parbat range, lying parallel to and north of the Rupal Valley, consists of a series of peaks with intervening dips. Some of these dips were dignified with the term pass, but this did not mean that they were in any way used by local inhabitants as passes. From east to west the Nanga Parbat range consists of Rakiot Peak (23,170 feet); Nanga Parbat (26,660 feet); Nanga Parbat Pass; Mazeno Peak (21,442 feet); Diamirai Pass; Diamirai Peak, and Gomar Singh Pass. The height of the base camp as estimated by Collie with a mercury barometer was 9,900 feet above sea level. Their objective, the summit of Nanga Parbat, therefore reared up almost 16,000 feet above their heads.

Chapter Five
Nanga Parbat II

Nanga Parbat II

On July 18, Mummery and Collie set off early, with the vague aim of climbing Chiche Peak (20,490 feet), on the south side of the valley. Such an ascent would give them a much better view of the Nanga Parbat range than could be obtained from base camp. Their first obstacle was the Nanga Parbat Glacier, sweeping down from the eternal ice cliffs on the south face of the mountain, at right angles to their path. A steep scramble up the mountainside brought them back into the Rupal valley. Proceeding up the valley they passed two more glaciers before aiming at a spot opposite the Chiche Glacier. Here Mummery and their native servant made several unsuccessful attempts to cross the Rupal torrent. Instead they ascended the valley to the point where the torrent arose from the Rupal Glacier, crossed over on the ice, and descended on the south bank to a campsite near the Chiche Glacier.

Their first close look at the south face of Nanga Parbat was not encouraging. The mountain rose almost sheer above them for 14,000 feet. A maze of rocky precipices, hanging glaciers and icy slopes, it appeared almost impregnable. One route, up a steep rock buttress, appeared to offer some hope of reaching the upper snow fields close to the Nanga Parbat Pass. Above the Pass they would still have to ascend 6000 feet. The biggest problem would be that of carrying supplies and equipment up this difficult route, for it was obvious several camps would have to be established in the bid for the summit.

Every bit as courageous as Mummery, Collie struck a much more cautious note in his appraisal of the difficulties facing them. He approached all his adventures with the attitude of the canny Scot as opposed to the impetuous, enthusiastic and optimistic Englishman. Before daylight the next morning they set off up the Chiche Glacier accompanied by the Kashmiri servants. Their only light was the faint gleam from candle lanterns. The ice was strewn with boulders and grooved with the debris of avalanches crashing down from above. As soon as the sun topped the surrounding ridges the glacier came to life. The ice creaked and groaned and the stones, loosened from their hold in the ice, bounced down the glacier. As the heat of the day closed in on them and the slope remorselessly steepened, their enthusiasm waned. A rocky spur on the right-hand side of the glacier offered an attractive alternative to floundering upwards in the snow and ice, but even this proved too much for their exhausted muscles. Accordingly they stopped for lunch at an altitude of 16,000 feet, much to the relief of their servants. This relief was short-lived, as their masters descended by the rocky spur, a feat which to the experienced mountaineer was a pleasure, but to the simple Kashmir men, all but impossible. Fortunately with the aid of the climbing rope the return journey was successfully accomplished. They reached the small camp beside the Chiche Glacier in the late afternoon to find that Hastings had come up to join them.

That evening a council of war was held. Their brief venture up the Chiche peak had convinced them that they were not yet in proper training. Hastings had brought a plentiful supply of provisions so that they were enabled to continue their explorations by climbing in a northwest direction from the Rupal Glacier, crossing the Nanga Parbat range and trying to swing round to the north of the range to survey the prospects there.

Early the next morning, July 20, before the sun had risen, the three climbers, accompanied by their servants and several coolies, set off for the Mazeno Pass. The route took them across the lower end of the Rupal Glacier, up its northern bank, across another glacier coming down at right angles from Nanga Parbat Pass and onto the Mazeno Glacier. The going was incredibly rough. The glaciers were deeply buried with rocky debris and severely crevassed. The moraine at the side was piled high with loose rocks, making any sustained or rhythmic pace impossible. The party crossed the upper part of the Mazeno Glacier in blazing sunshine, and after an exhausting struggle over rocks and soft snow, gained the summit of the Pass. Collie was seized with an attack of mountain sickness so violent that he was scarcely able to crawl to the top. The descent on the other side of the Pass was steep and their movements slow. They were overtaken by night at the edge of the Lubar Glacier, so named for a tiny shepherd's encampment at its lower end.

The next morning they purchased some gourds of dirty goat's milk and a sheep before bearing off to their right around the northern slopes of the Nanga Parbat range. They were now aiming for the Diamirai Valley, which was filled with its own glacier, and occupied roughly the same position on the north as the Rupal Valley occupied on the south side of the range. Two ridges separated them from the Diamirai Valley, but they were ridges of Himalayan proportions. A comfortable camp was set up on the hillside by a small stream, at an altitude of 12,500 feet. As evening closed in they had a magnificent view to the west over country untravelled by Europeans, to giant snow peaks at the head of the Swat Valley.

A rugged five-hour walk the next day brought them to a campsite on the south side of the Diamirai Glacier. To the east they could see the towering mass of Nanga Parbat, 14,000 feet above them. Mummery soon pointed out a route by which he hoped later to gain the upper snow field, just underneath the summit, and thence the topmost pinnacle which glistened in the sunlight. The food supplies were almost exhausted, however, and they were forced to return to base camp. The servants were sent back by the route they had travelled crossing the Mazeno Pass. Mummery suggested that to avoid the tedium of that route, the three climbers should cross the Nanga Parbat range by ascending the north face in the region of the Diamirai Peak, and descend the south face onto the Mazeno Glacier, or even with good luck onto the Rupal Glacier. Their experience over the next forty-eight hours provided them with their first real insight into the formidable nature of Himalayan exploration.

Mummery, Collie, and Hastings set out at midnight by the light of candles, and stumbled interminably over boulders until they reached a rocky arête. This they climbed in a depressing mist which settled on the mountainside at 11 a.m. Finally they reached a ridge which led to the top of a peak on the west side of the Diamirai Pass; about 1000 feet above the ridge (to avoid the fatigue of climbing this peak), they launched out onto the exposed southern face of the mountain. At one point they crossed a great amphitheatre of soft snow resting on a steep ice slope. The danger of avalanching was great, but by spreading themselves out on the one hundred and forty feet of rope, they safely passed across. The Diamirai Pass (18,050 feet), was reached at 2 p.m., but their congratulations turned to dismay when they could see neither the Rupal Valley nor the Mazeno Pass. Easy rocks and snow led down to a small glacier, which eventually turned westward to the Lubar Glacier. In fourteen hours they had travelled three miles as the crow flies, had climbed 6000 feet, but were now far below the Mazeno Pass, on the wrong side, and were in fact back near their campsite of two nights before.

Quickly they descended to the Lubar Glacier, and at 5:30 p.m. started on the long exhausting climb up the Mazeno Pass. Their food was reduced to a slice of meat, some sticks of chocolate and about six biscuits. Collie acknowledged his eternal gratitude to pipe tobacco: "I shall never forget how tobacco helped me through that night, as I smoked whilst waiting on the summit, in the freezing air and the bright starlight, for Mummery and Hastings; it almost made me feel that I was enjoying myself; and it stayed the pangs of hunger and soothed away the utter weariness that beset both mind and body."[1] Daylight found them struggling down the Mazeno Glacier. By this time Collie and Hastings were well in front and found a Kashmiri servant waiting for them at the end of the glacier with a fire and supplies of food. At 10:30 a.m. on July 24, Collie pushed on to send ponies back to help Mummery and Hastings return to base camp. Collie arrived at base camp at 6 p.m. To his delight Bruce had arrived on a month's leave from the army, bringing with him two Ghurkhas, Ragobir and Gomar Singh.

Bruce at this time was a major in the Indian Army, though he later, after a distinguished career of soldiering and mountaineering, rose to the rank of General. He had a tremendous sense of humour and delighted in telling a good story against himself. For this reason he was very popular in camp. His laugh was loud and irresistible and his friends said that whether you heard the joke or not, even if you were in another room, you had to laugh too. Always a robust man, as can be seen from Collie's photographs taken in 1895, Bruce spent much of his life fighting against obesity.

On July 26, while Collie and Bruce were teaching the Ghurkhas to climb on ice and snow, Mummery wrote to his wife describing their recent ordeal:

> Camp life out here is a great spree. One has every luxury, and men run errands, and fetch and carry at every turn. So far we have had a little climb on a small rock peak. Crossed the Mazeno Pass (a native pass); crossed into the Diamirai valley (uninhabited but beautiful in the extreme); glorious trees (mostly birch and pine); thickets of wild roses; heaps of flowers and undergrowth.
>
> After a day's rest we came back by a very long pass, affording one or two bits of interesting rock climbing. Unluckily it led up the wrong side of the chain and we had to finish up with recrossing the Mazeno, as we had no food reserves. We were from 15,000 to 18,000 feet up all day long, and felt as fresh as daisies, so I don't think we are going to be bothered much by the rarity of the air. We discovered an absolutely safe way up Nanga. Easy glacier up which coolies can carry our camp, and thence onward, a broad snow and rock ridge right up to the top.[2]

That same day, Mummery wrote a more serious letter to a future President of the Alpine Club, in which he admitted that "on our first pass, the Mazeno, we felt very bad partly from interminable loose stones, and partly from rarity of air."[3]

On July 27 Mummery, Collie, Bruce and the two Ghurkhas climbed Tashing Peak by ascending the glacier behind the village of Tashing. To the northeast they observed masses of snow-clad peaks, one of which stood out higher than the others. This was the Mustagh Tower about fifty miles distant. They camped out for the night and returned to base camp by a different route. The next day was spent preparing to return to the Diamirai Valley on the north, as Mummery had by now given up all thought of attempting the south face of Nanga Parbat. All subsequent expeditions to the mountain were made from the north.

On July 30, Gomar Singh was sent ahead with the servants and all their supplies by the well-explored route over the Mazeno Pass. Mummery, Collie, Hastings, Bruce and Ragobir were to try a direct crossing of the Nanga Parbat range from the head of the Rupal Valley to the head of the Diamirai Valley. Collie had some misgivings about this project, but Mummery's enthusiasm overcame all objections. They camped for the night at 13,000 feet, about four miles short of the Mazeno Pass. Early next morning they set off in the dark up an excessively steep moraine, alternating with glaciers, rock ridges and snow couloirs. By 3 p.m. Bruce, who was suffering from the early effects of mumps, was so tired that he had to be revived with caffeine citrate lozenges. Two hours later, after a climb of 7000 feet, they had almost reached the summit on the ridge of 21,442 feet. But they were also very tired and Collie, Bruce and Ragobir after their evening meal retreated downward in the direction of the Mazeno Glacier. Night overtook them at 19,000 feet. Tied together on a rocky ledge, they perched for the night. Daylight on August 1 found them struggling up the Mazeno Pass with Collie and Ragobir in the lead. On the way down the west side of the Pass, Ragobir, who had not eaten for forty-eight hours, collapsed. Collie sat with him smoking his pipe until the rest of the party joined them later in the day. Slowly they struggled down the Lubar Glacier, Collie remaining behind to accompany Mummery who was very tired. As the sun was setting they arrived at the shepherds' settlement at Lubar, to see Bruce

seated on the small wall in his shirt sleeves, superintending the slaughter of one of the sheep. And horrible to relate, in less than half an hour after we entered Lubar we were all ravenously devouring pieces of sheep liver only half cooked on the ends of sticks. The dirty, sour goat's milk, too was delicious and as far as I can recollect each of us drank considerably over a gallon that evening, to wash down the fragments of toasted sheep and chappatties that we made from some flour that providentially remained behind our caravan with a sick coolie.[4]

The next day they continued on to the new base camp on the southern edge of the Diamirai Glacier.

August 4 and 5 were spent resting in camp. Mummery took the opportunity of writing a letter to his wife to be taken out by Bruce on his return journey to Abbottabad. In this letter he made light of their recent harrowing experiences. He referred, however, to the effect of the thin air on their systems. "There is no mistake about the rarity of the air," he wrote, "it touches one no end."[5] The tone of the letter was a little more guarded than his previous correspondence. He even suggested that the trip would have been worthwhile even if they did not reach the summit of Nanga Parbat. Such a thought would have been unthinkable two weeks earlier when the expedition first arrived at the foot of the mountain. There is little doubt that a combination of fatigue, the effects of altitude and the realization of the enormity of their task had exerted a dampening effect on Mummery's usually effervescent spirits.

Bruce departed on August 5, leaving behind the two Ghurkhas to act as high altitude porters. During the next few days various explorations were carried out. Mummery and Ragobir managed to reach the top of the second rib of rocks directly under the summit, at a height of about 18,000 feet. This was an exhilarating piece of climbing. With the exception of a greatly distorted glacier between the first and second rock ribs, and an exposed couloir swept by avalanches, the route led over great slabs and towers of rock set at a very steep angle. Meanwhile Collie with Gomar Singh and their Kashmir shikari explored the east end of the Diamirai Glacier, ascending a ridge to the northeast overlooking the Diama Glacier. On August 7, they were confined to camp by heavy rain, but during the next two days, Mummery, Collie, Ragobir and Lhor Khan (a local native porter) carried a waterproof bag of provisions and some other supplies to a height of 17,150 feet, on the route reconnoitred by Mummery. Coolies carried quantities of fuel up to a lower altitude. The supplies included 12 pounds of chocolate, 6 tins of Huntley and Palmer's biscuits, Brand's soups and essence.

By now the three climbers were wearied by the altitude and their continuous exertions. Collie and Mummery were still able to climb, but Hastings was laid up with an injured heel. The weather had turned worse with heavy rain at the base camp and snow higher on the mountain. They would need a week of fine weather before it would be safe to climb again. Food was running short. Provisions which had been ordered from Srinagar had never arrived. Accordingly Hastings, aided by the porters, generously agreed to make his way out to Astor where he might find fresh supplies or locate the missing ones. He discovered a variation of the route over the range by traversing a pass, named eponymously after his orderly the Gomar Singh Pass, at the western end of the Nanga Parbat range.

On August 11, having seen Hastings safely on his way, Mummery, Collie, Ragobir and Lhor Khan climbed the Diamirai Peak (19,000 feet). This strenuous climb, the last 3000 feet of which Collie described as very severe, was led throughout by Mummery, who cut steps in the ice for most of the route. At one point near the summit they moved out onto the mountain face over a sensational precipice. In attempting to regain the ridge Lhor Khan fell off, but was held on the rope by Collie and Ragobir. With great presence of mind he pulled himself back onto the ice steps and continued the climb not in the least upset by his brush with death. It is impossible not to be impressed by the courage and cheerfulness of Lhor Khan. A simple peasant, he was engaged in a climb of the highest technical calibre for the first time in his life. For footwear he had some wet sheep-skin wrapped around his legs.

When they reached the summit at 11:30 a.m., Collie and Lhor Khan were suffering from fatigue and headaches. Collie expressed his concern that the effects of altitude at 26,600 feet, the summit of Nanga Parbat, might be overwhelming, but his arguments had little effect on Mummery, who laughed at his concern. At 1 p.m. they started downward by a rock ridge to the west. This led them into a formidable chimney coated with ice and finally in heavy mist they lost their way. After coming out on the south side of the main range, they had to climb back up over the range at the Gomar Singh Pass. It was not until long after dark that they reached camp in the Diamirai Valley.

This episode demonstrates quite forcibly how slow Mummery was to realize the dangers they were facing on their climbing expedition. They had now got lost or gone badly astray on three occasions. In their own way, they were only following the traditional methods of Alpine climbing, a one or two day all-out assault on a peak. The technique of future Himalayan expeditions—a slow build-up, over several weeks, with camps on the route to the summit—lay about thirty years in the future. Nevertheless their luck, especially with the weather, was fantastic.

After being kept in camp one day by heavy rain, at 2 a.m. on August 15, Collie, Mummery, Ragobir, Lhor Khan and a coolie set off for the upper depot, carrying firewood, provisions and a silk tent. By the time they arrived at the top of the glacier, Collie was suffering from a severe headache, and turned back. For some time he watched Mummery, Ragobir and Lhor Khan clinging like flies to the rocks high above him. Then he returned wearily down the glacier to camp. Mummery meanwhile camped out above the second rib of rock, where he picked up their earlier cache of supplies. The next day, entirely in mist, he climbed up another 1000 feet, onto a third rib of rock, where he left a rucksack of food. As darkness settled down on the mountain and rain began to fall, Collie anxiously awaited his return.

> But later in the dark, he marched back into camp, entirely wet through, but far more cheerful than the circumstances warranted, and very pleased with the climbing. His account of the ice world on Nanga Parbat was wonderful. No-where in the Caucasus had he seen anything to compare with it. . . . The crevasses were enormous,and the rock climbing, although difficult, was set at such a steep angle, that no time would be lost in making height towards the upper glacier underneath the final peak. If only the weather would clear, Mummery was sure that we could get onto this upper glacier.[6]

But the weather closed in, and for the next two days the camp was beset by a violent blizzard. When it cleared, Mummery was keen for an immediate assault, as the native porters predicted more bad weather. Collie reluctantly agreed, and on August 18, Mummery, Ragobir, and Collie set off up to the head of the Diama Glacier. Here at 15,000 feet they erected camp with adequate firewood and provisions. Further up the mountain at the third rib of rocks was a rucksack of food. The next morning, Collie was ill with indigestion from the coarse flour they had been eating, and he returned to base camp. Two nights later Mummery returned. He had spent the first night above the second rib of rocks. The next day, August 20, he started with Ragobir before daylight, and climbed up the third rock rib to the upper snow field. The climbing was excessively difficult, but appeared to get easier the higher they climbed. Finally at a little over 20,000 feet, Ragobir became ill and Mummery, realizing at last that to spend another night on the mountain would probably be fatal, turned back. This was a great disappointment to him, as it virtually ended his attempts to reach the summit.

Hastings arrived at base camp the next day with ample provisions, so that fresh plans could be made. Mummery regretfully decided to abandon the attempt on Nanga Parbat from the Diamirai Glacier. They agreed that their final chance lay on the Rakiot Glacier to the east, where perhaps the ascent would be less precipitous. This was a wise decision, as subsequent expeditions succeeded in climbing the mountain from this glacier. Collie and Hastings would take the main body of servants, coolies, and supplies by an easy route over the Red Pass to the north. Mummery with Ragobir and Gomar Singh would retrieve their supplies high up on the mountain, and proceed over the Diama Glacier, by the Diama Pass to the Rakiot Glacier. On August 23, Mummery sat down to write his last letter to his wife.

> Our chances of bagging the peak look badly enough. Collie is not keen on it, and old Hastings has managed to get a chill, so I am left with the Ghurkas. They are first rate climbers and good men, but I cannot afford the help of a real A.C. [Alpine Club] man. Well, I shall soon be on my way home; you must not be too disappointed about Nanga.
>
> I have had some slap-up climbs, and seen cliffs and séracs such as the Alps and Caucasus cannot touch. Nanga on this side is 12,000 feet of rock and ice as steep and difficult as a series of Matterhorns and Mont Blancs piled one on another. I should have got up, I fancy if Ragobir (a Ghurka) had not got ill at a critical moment, and I had to see him down. There is no doubt the air affects us when we get beyond 18,000 feet. To-morrow I cross a high pass with the Ghurkas to the Rakiot Glacier. Hastings and Collie go round with the coolies and stores. If the N.W. side of Nanga is easy we may yet pull it off, but you will have a wire before this reaches you.[7]

Ragobir and Gomar Singh were sent ahead to retrieve the supplies from the high altitude camp. Mummery set off with Lhor Khan and Rosamir, the head coolie, to meet the two Ghurkhas on the Diama Pass. The next morning, August 24, 1895, Lhor Khan and Rosamir watched the other three set off up the Diama Pass to the east. Mummery, Ragobir and Gomar Singh were never seen again.

The realization of the tragedy was slow to develop. Collie and Hastings, with the remainder of the porters, had set off on August 23, heading north across the Diamirai Glacier. They ascended the opposite side of the valley by a route which took them through the Red Pass, about 16,000 feet, to the east of Gonar Peak. A laborious descent followed on the icy slopes to

*Nanga Parbat. The dotted line shows the route
to the highest camp (X) on Nanga Parbat*

the north of the Pass, and it was night before they arrived at a spot where they could collect enough wood for fires and erect the tent. The next day was long and exhausting, as they pushed across the Ganolo Glacier and up a steep hillside in an attempt to reach the Rakiot Glacier, but they were forced to camp on the hillside. On August 25, they crossed a pass of about 16,500 feet into the Rakiot Valley, where in a thunderstorm and amidst dripping trees they set up camp on the near side of the Rakiot Glacier. The prospect was cheerless. Collie records that:

> from the top of the last pass we had come over, we could see the great face down which Mummery and the Ghurkas would have had to come had they reached the Diama Pass. It seemed to us quite hopeless. I spent about half an hour looking through a powerful telescope for any trace of steps cut down the only ridge that looked at all feasible. I could see none. Hastings and I were therefore of the opinion that Mummery had turned back. This he had told us he intended to do should he find the pass either dangerous or very difficult, for, as he pointed out, he was not going to risk anything on an ordinary pass.[8]

As Mummery had three days' food supply with him, Collie and Hastings did not become anxious about him until August 29, when a search of the Rakiot and Ganolo Glaciers revealed no traces of the missing men. Hastings agreed to return to the Diamirai Valley to continue the search, and Collie, who was due back in England by the end of September, hastened over the mountains to Astor where he could telegraph the military posts along the Gilgit road.

Collie received a telegram from Hastings on September 5. Hastings had climbed up to the spot where Lhor Khan and Rosamir waved goodbye to Mummery and the two Ghurkhas as they set off for the Diama Pass. He had recovered some provisions left behind by Mummery as a reserve in case the pass should prove impracticable. As the party had never returned for these provisions, some castrophe must have overtaken them during their attempt to climb over the pass. On September 13, Collie and Hastings reunited at the small military post of Bunar on the Indus. From here it took three days of hard travelling to reach the site of their second base camp in the Diamirai Valley. The wind was cold and the leaves were swept from the trees. The ground was powdered with snow. Winter had settled in at this high altitude just as the natives had warned it would. But Collie made one last attempt to look for his friend.

Hastings and I soon saw that any attempt at exploration amongst the higher glaciers was out of the question. We went up the glacier as far as halfway to the old upper camp where the provisions had been found untouched, but even there it was wading through snow nearly a foot deep; ultimately we climbed through heavy powdery snow, perhaps 500 feet up the south side of the valley, to obtain a last look at the valley in which Mummery, Ragobir and Gomar Singh had perished. The avalanches were thundering down the face of Nanga Parbat, filling the air with their dust; and if nothing else had made it impossible to penetrate into the fastness of the cold, cheerless, and snow-covered mountain-land, they at least spoke with no uncertain voice, and bade us begone. Slowly we descended, and for the last time looked on the great mountain and the white snows where in some unknown spot our friends lay buried.[9]

The effect of this tragedy on the mountaineering world was profound, but because of the remote area in which it occurred, the first report in the press did not appear until November 12, 1895. On that date the London *Times* published a one and a half column obituary, probably written by Collie. This in itself was an indication of the public concern over the death of Mummery. In some ways the loss of Mummery was like that of George Leigh-Mallory and Andrew Irvine on the northeast ridge of Everest in 1914. Both Mummery and Mallory were amongst the outstanding climbers of their day. Both disappeared with scarcely a trace. On June 13, 1939, Hans Lobenhoffer and Ludwig Chicken followed Mummery's route over the rock ribs above the Diamirai ice fall. They came on the historic campsite on top of the second rib of rock and found a small log of wood, which could only have been brought there by the hand of man, and which had lain there undisturbed for almost half a century. In the Everest expedition of 1933, Wyn Harris and Lawrence Wager, at a height of about 28,000 feet on the northeast ridge, recovered an ice axe which could only have belonged to Mallory and Irvine.

Mummery's contribution to Himalayan climbing has received little recognition. He was the first climber to mount an expedition on a single Himalayan peak. His only predecessors in this field of mountaineering had been the Schlagintweit brothers in 1858 and W.W. Graham with his Swiss guides in 1883. Mummery's expedition involved not only pioneer climbing, but pioneer exploration as well. He trained native coolies to be high altitude porters of the highest calibre. The performance of Lhor Khan was quite outstanding and antedated the use of Sherpa porters by about thirty years. Major Bruce's introduction of Ghurkha soldiers from Nepal as high-level porters was an innovation which was to be taken up by later

Himalayan expeditions. Collie's detailed account of the expedition and Mummery's letters drew attention to the marked deterioration in performance above an altitude of 18,000 feet, although the cause of this deterioration was attributed to thin air or in Collie's opinion, to a bacillus causing infections at high altitudes. The problem of supplies caused great difficulty to Mummery's expedition. He had hoped to rely on native produce, but this was hard to obtain even for an expedition as small as his. In any case the lack of supplies required the periodic withdrawal of one of the climbers to the native villages. Subsequent Himalayan expeditions took their own supplies with them.

Collie never returned to the Himalaya and he maintained a complete silence about the question of whether Mummery had taken unjustifiable risks. There is little doubt that, by present-day standards, the risks taken were quite horrifying. But at the time many of these risks were unknown, and although Collie had expressed grave concern about the effects of high altitude and doubts about the wisdom of the final attempt on Nanga Parbat, he faithfully supported his leader to the end.

After the death of Mummery, Collie emerged as a leader of mountaineering expeditions in his own right. His training had been hard and varied, first on British hills and then in the Alps where he participated in the Silver Age of British mountaineering. The Alpine climbs of Mummery, Collie, Hastings and Slingsby set the standards for generations of British and European climbers. Finally, Collie was hardened on the icy slopes of Nanga Parbat, so that when he entered the field of Canadian mountaineering in 1897, he came as one of the foremost British practitioners of that exacting sport.

Chapter Six
The Canadian Rockies
1897-1898

The Canadian Rockies 1897-1898

When Collie accepted the invitation of Professor Charles E. Fay of Boston to join the Appalachian Club for a climbing season in the Canadian Rockies in 1897, he opened up for himself one of the most fruitful and enjoyable phases of his mountaineering career. In company with other leading climbers of his generation, he had been casting around for new peaks to conquer. The Alps had been challenging, but the finding of new routes up old peaks could be left to the younger generation. Remote as they were, the Caucasus had been explored by several members of the Alpine Club. The Himalaya were much more remote, travel was severely restricted by political considerations, and the tragic loss of Mummery ruled out a return to Nanga Parbat for anyone as sensitive as Collie. The most tempting field for new mountaineering was the vast range of the Rocky Mountains, the backbone of the American continent, which had only recently become accessible with the passage of the railroads across Canada.

Collie's interest in the Canadian Rockies was no doubt stimulated by the fact that the height of the mountains was largely unknown. He shared the common misconception as to the altitudes of Mount Brown and Mount Hooker, which David Douglas had reported to be between 16,000 and 17,000 feet. In 1814 Douglas, an energetic Scottish botanist, had been sent by Sir William Hooker and the Royal Horticultural Society to spend a few seasons botanising on the Pacific coast of North America. Three years later, while crossing the Athabasca Pass with the spring fur brigade, he outdistanced the rest of the party and arrived at the Committee Punch Bowl on the summit. He noted two peaks guarding the pass; the one on the west he named Mount Brown in honour of R. Brown, a distinguished botanist, and the one on the east he named Mount Hooker after his patron at the University of Glasgow.

In his field journal entry for May 1, 1827, Douglas described his ascent of Mount Brown:

> After breakfast at one o'clock being as I conceived at the highest part of the route, I became desirous of ascending one of the peaks, and accordingly I set out alone on snowshoes to that on the left hand or west side (of Athabasca Pass), being to all appearance the highest. The labour of ascending the lower part, which is covered with pines, is great beyond description, sinking on many occasions to the middle. Half-way up vegetation ceases entirely, not so much as a vestige of moss or lichen on the stones. One-third from the summit it becomes a mountain of pure ice, sealed over by Nature's Hand, a momentous work of Nature's God. The height from its base may be about 5,500 feet; timber 2,750; a few mosses and lichens, 500 more; 1,000 feet of perpetual snow; the remainder, toward the top, 1,250, as I have said, glacier with a thin covering of snow on it. The ascent took me five hours; descending only one hour and a quarter.[1]

Douglas made no scientific observations to confirm his estimated height of Mount Brown at between 16,000 and 17,000 feet. His description of the proportions covered by timber, mosses, snow and ice, was fairly accurate, however, as confirmed by L.Q. Coleman and L.B. Stewart when they climbed it in 1893. Part of the error in Douglas' estimation lay in the fact that Lieutenant Aemilius Simpson during his survey from Jasper House in the winter of 1825-26 had incorrectly calculated the altitude of the Athabasca Pass as 11,000 feet. The true height of the pass is 5,724 feet and Mount Brown 9,156 feet. Douglas had therefore only climbed 3,400 feet above the pass. Whatever the cause of the error, maps published after 1829 showed a height of 17,000 feet for Mount Brown and 16,000 feet for Mount Hooker. Furthermore the peaks were shown as lying north and south of the pass, whereas on modern maps they lie east and west. L.Q. Coleman did not completely clear up the mystery; although he identified and climbed Mount Brown, he failed to identify the Mount Hooker described by Douglas. The myth of the 17,000 foot mountain provided a tremendous stimulus to future mountaineers and greatly hastened their footsteps northward from Lake Louise. Certainly in 1897 the myth influenced Norman Collie in his decision to return to Canada in future years; from the summit of Mount Freshfield he noted that "far away—perhaps thirty miles to the north-west a magnificent snow-covered mountain was to be seen—from the way it towered above its neighbours it seemed excessively high—there were only two peaks of that size, and so far north, marked on the maps. These were Brown and Hooker, reputed to be 16,000 and 15,700 feet high. . . . "[2]

The birth of mountaineering as a sport in Canada probably took place about 1888 when the Reverend W.S. Green and H. Swanzy, members of the Alpine Club, visited the Selkirks. Green's book *Among the Selkirk Glaciers* aroused much interest in the newly discovered Canadian Switzerland. In 1890 two members of the Swiss Alpine Club made the first ascent of Mount Sir Donald, the most conspicuous peak in the Selkirks, and as it was close to the railway at Glacier House it became a most popular climb. In 1893 W.D. Wilcox and S.E.S. Allen, both students at Yale, commenced a valuable series of explorations in the region of the Great Divide, opening up country from Fortress Lake in the north to the Kananaskis River including Mount Assiniboine in the south. Wilcox was a wonderful photographer and his book *The Rockies of Canada* (1900) was widely acclaimed and to this day preserves a freshness of style which makes it one of the outstanding books from this early period of mountaineering.

In 1894 the Appalachian Mountain Club of Boston headed by its energetic president, Professor Charles Fay, made its first appearance in the Canadian Rockies. Over the next few years its members concentrated on exploration and climbing in the Lake Louise area. Allen, Frissell and Wilcox's climb of Mount Temple (11,626 feet) was the first ascent of a major Canadian peak. The next year an Appalachian Club party consisting of Professor Fay, Charles S. Thompson and Philip S. Abbot made the first ascent of Mount Hector (11,135 feet). Abbot described the view from Mount Hector as one which "cannot be matched in any other mountain system in the world except in Asia."[3] Mount Hector, situated on the eastern shoulder of the Banff-Jasper Highway, near Lake Louise, is today the most accessible of the major peaks. Within two minutes of parking an automobile at the roadside, the climber is on the lower slopes, and the ascent, although strenuous, is technically easy if the snow conditions are right.

Collie's New World mountaineering was an indirect result of the first disaster in the Canadian Rockies. On August 3, 1896, a party of four men, Professor Fay, P.S. Abbot, C.S. Thompson and the Reverend George Little, set out to climb Mount Lefroy, a magnificent peak situated at the far end of Lake Louise. Mount Lefroy on the left and Mount Victoria on the right close in the far end of Lake Louise. The two peaks are separated by a formidable gorge, now known as the "Death Trap," into which avalanches pour off the Victoria Glacier. Up this cleft, however, lies the route which leads to the summit of the Abbot Pass (9000 feet), a suitable take-off point for the attempt on Mount Lefroy or Mount Victoria. The climbers did not leave the Lake Louise Chalet until 6:15 a.m., a late hour for the problems which lay ahead. Toiling up the ice slopes of the gorge, the four men reached the Abbot Pass at noon. After a short pause for lunch they set off up the remaining 2000 feet of steep ice slopes, their frequent step-cutting interspersed with careful advances over unreliable rock. At 5:30 p.m. the party drew under an immense rocky bastion, possibly seventy-five feet high, behind which lay the summit. Pressed for time, they abandoned the safer route onto the north ridge because of the prolonged step-cutting that would be required in the steep ice. Instead Abbot, moving along the rock wall, found a narrow vertical cleft up which he scrambled. The others unroped and stood aside to avoid the shower of loose stones he sent down. Further up he traversed a short ledge to the left before entering a gully. A moment later he fell to his death 900 feet below.

This disaster led to the abandonment of all mountaineering that year, but prompted Professor Fay to bring back a strong party the next year to complete the climb. To further his plans, he invited the Alpine Club of London to send a contingent to join them. Collie and Professor H.B. Dixon of Manchester accepted, taking with them Peter Sarbach of St. Niklaus, the first Swiss guide to climb in Canada. Towards the end of July 1897, the climbing party assembled at Glacier House in the Selkirk range of British Columbia. As well as Collie, Dixon and Sarbach, it included Fay, A. Michael, H.C. Parker, the Rev. C.L. Noyes and J.R. Vanderlip. Several peaks in the Selkirks were climbed before the party returned to Laggan (the original name of the railway station for Lake Louise) where they were joined by Thompson. At Lake Louise they were welcomed to the wooden chalet built by the C.P.R. to accommodate tourists and climbers. Here they came under the special attention of Mr. Howard, the chef, who provided a regular hot breakfast at 3 a.m. with juicy beefsteaks, hot rolls and coffee, and sat up all night to make certain the arrangements were perfect.

After the meal they crept out into the starlight to the rowboat *Agnes*, and stowing their belongings in the bow, pushed off to be rowed across the lake by the slow steady strokes of Michael and Sarbach. The day was August 3, 1897, the anniversary of Philip Abbot's death. To Collie they seemed to be "travelling through some forgotten land, a land of old

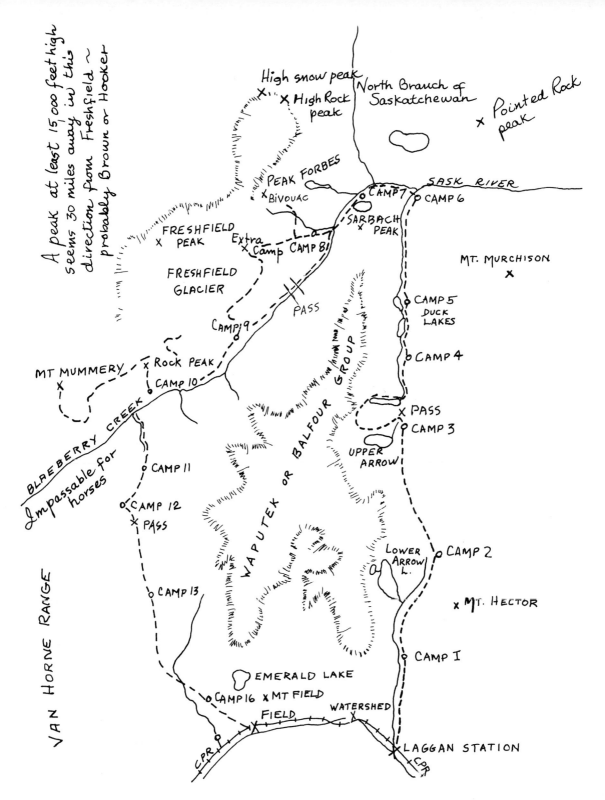

Sketch map drawn by Collie and attached to letter dated October 2, 1897.

romance, where high above, perched on the almost inaccessible crags, is the castle of the lord of the valley, a land where knights in armour rescue fair ladies from imprisonment, and roam abroad in search of perilous adventures."[4]

This romantic spell was quickly broken, for after disembarking in darkness the party was soon struggling through rushing streams, thickets of willows, fallen trees and huge stones. This miniature jungle soon gave way to the Victoria Glacier, which in time led up the steep snow slopes of the "Death Trap". A long remorseless uphill grind of the kind that deters all but the most determined mountaineer brought the party out onto the snowy col of the Abbot Pass five hours after leaving the boat.

Their route to the summit of Lefroy followed that of the previous year. The steep slope was divided into three sections by two bands of rotten limestone ledges. Fortunately the snow was in good condition; firm enough to kick steps in, but not so hard as to require cutting. The real difficulty and danger lay above the second band of rocks where they were soon confronted by the cliff which Abbot had tried to scale. This they avoided by kicking a ladder of snow steps up a gully between the rock and the utterly exposed ice face on which the snow no longer lay. A snow arête led upwards from the top of the cliff to the summit cornice, and at 11 a.m. they reached the highest point of Mount Lefroy.

In the clear air under a cloudless sky the view was magnificent, a perfect introduction to the Canadian Rockies for the British visitors. Near at hand the striking peak of Hungabee presented a first-rate challenge to future climbers. Far to the south the black precipices of Mount Assiniboine were clearly visible. Tucked away in the pine forests far below was Lake O'Hara, and fifteen miles to the north Mount Balfour, rising out of the Waputik snow field, presented a challenge which they hoped to take up in a few days. But with the threat of the sun melting the steps in the snow there was no time to linger, and reluctantly they began the descent. They were back on the Abbot Pass by 3 p.m., and two and a half hours later at Lake Louise. No doubt the remarkable Mr. Howard was waiting with suitable food and drink to restore the diminished energies of the successful climbers.

After a day of rest Collie, Fay, Michael, and Sarbach on August 5, returned to attempt Mount Victoria. Collie was asked to lead the climbers, the Swiss guide gracefully yielding his usual place to his distinguished patron. Again an early start was made under the starlight. Now that the best route was known, much better progress was made to the Abbot Pass.

Here turning to the right instead of the left, as had been done on the ascent of Lefroy, height was rapidly gained by climbing a series of small terraces of excessively rotten rocks. During occasional halts, the snow-slope of Lefroy, up which the larger party had so labouriously toiled forty-eight hours previously, could be seen, now converted by the two days' fine weather into an iceslope, which, further off to the right, fell away with great steepness to the head of the Lake O'Hara valley. The long arête of Mount Victoria that can be seen against the sky from the chalet at Lake Louise, was soon reached. The climbing along the arête was not difficult but required care, and it was only the last five hundred feet that were at all narrow. About midday, after breaking many steps in soft snow, the summit was finally reached—a small pinnacle of snow, 11,500 feet (now 11,365) above sea-level.[5]

They spent an exhilarating half hour on the summit, photographing, measuring, and admiring the magnificent peaks of Hungabee, Neptuak, Lefroy Temple, Huber and Goodsir. Signals made to the chalet far below them went unnoticed even though watchers had been studying the peak with telescopes. Reluctantly leaving the summit they returned the way they had come, pausing to drink from a small blue lakelet in the ice below the crest and cooking a celebratory meal of boned turkey over an ether-fed stove on Abbot Pass. They disembarked from the *Agnes* at 5:30 p.m. to receive the congratulations of the company gathered at the chalet.

Two days later on August 7, the combined American and British party, augmented by the arrival of G.P. Baker, set off up the Bow Valley in search of Mount Balfour. Their guide was Bill Peyto, for whom Peyto Lake is named. W.D. Wilcox has left this description of Peyto, one of the most colorful men in his trade.

Bill is very quiet in civilisation, but becomes more communicative around an evening campfire, when he delights to tell his adventures. His life has been a roving life. The story of his battle with the world, his escapades and sufferings of hunger and exposure, not to mention the dreams and ambitions of a keen imagination with their consequent disappointments, has served to entertain many an evening hour. Peyto assumes a wild and picturesque though somewhat tattered attire. A sombrero, with a rakish tilt to one side, a blue shirt set off by a white kerchief (which may have served civilisation for a napkin), and a buck-skin coat with a fringed border, add to his cowboy appearance. A heavy belt containing a row of cartridges, hunting-knife and six-shooter as well as the restless activity of his wicked blue eyes, give him an air of bravado. He usually wears two pairs of trousers, one over the other, the outer pair about six months older. This was shown by their dilapidated and faded state, hanging, after a week of rough work in burnt timber, in a tattered fringe knee-high. Every once in a while Peyto would give one or two nervous yanks at the fringe and tear off the longer pieces, so that his outer trousers disappeared day by day from below upwards. Part of this was affectation, to impress the tenderfoot, or the "dude," as he calls everyone who wears a collar. But in spite of this Peyto is one of the most conscientious and experienced men with horses that I have ever known. [6]

Peyto set off early with the main party, leaving three Indian ponies behind for the rear party of Collie, Fay and Baker. These three were inexperienced woodsmen, and it was only with the help of a man at Laggan railway station that they managed to load the refractory steeds with a mound of baggage. They then followed what for want of a better term was called the trail, but in reality consisted of a tortuous route over fallen trees, through willow thickets and into endless swamps or muskegs. Peyto had carefully blazed the trail by marking the trees, but late in the day they lost sight of the blazes and followed instead the old upright poles of the railway survey carried out five years before. This led them into a muskeg where one pony all but disappeared into a deep hole. The three climbers rescued him by removing his pack and pulling him out with alpine ropes. Finally at 11 p.m. Fay floundered ahead to reach camp. Peyto returned to guide Collie and Baker, very likely subjecting them to caustic comments about dudes.

After this humiliating start, conditions improved. The party established a pleasant camp beside upper Bow Lake, in beautiful open country surrounded by fine mountains and glaciers. On August 10, they climbed the glacier at the end of Bow Lake and after a long hike over the upper snow fields arrived at the summit of Mount Gordon, which they had mistaken for Mount Balfour. All around them stretched snow-covered unnamed peaks. While resting they named Mount Collie, Mount Baker and Mount Thompson. Further to the west a flat-topped mountain was given the name Mount Mummery in memory of Collie's friend. After spending some time on the summit, the party set off for a second summit about one third of a mile to the westward.

It was near the top of the second peak that Thompson very nearly ended his climbing career. Collie described the accident:

Not far from this second summit a huge crevasse partially covered with snow had to be crossed. All the party had passed over but Thompson, who unfortunately broke through and at once disappeared headlong into the great crack that ran perpendicularly down into the depths of the glacier. Those of the party who were still on the first peak saw their friends gesticulating in the far distance, but did not take much notice until Sarbach drew their attention to the fact that there were only four people instead of five to be seen: someone therefore must have fallen down a crevasse. A race across the almost level snow then took place, Sarbach being easily first. Although Thompson was too far down to be seen, yet he could be heard calling for help and saying that although he was not hurt, he would be extremely grateful to us if we could make haste and extricate him from the awkward position he was in, for he could not move and was almost upside down, jammed between the two opposing sides of the crevasse.[7]

It was obvious that every second was of importance. A stirrup was made in a rope, and Collie, the lightest member of the party and unmarried, put his foot into it, while he was carefully roped round the waist as well. Then he was pushed over the edge of the abyss, and swung in mid-air. To quote his description:

I was then lowered into the gaping hole. On one side the ice fell sheer, on the other it was undercut, but again bulged outwards about eighteen feet below the surface, making the crevasse at that point not much more than two feet wide. Then it widened again, and went down into dim twilight. It was not till I had descended sixty feet, almost the whole available length of an eighty foot rope, that at last I became tightly wedged between the two walls of the crevasse, and was absolutely incapable of moving my body. My feet were close to Thompson's, but his head was further away, and about three feet lower than his heel. Face downwards, and covered with fallen snow, he could not see me. But, after he explained that it was entirely his own fault that he was there, I told him we would have him out in no time. At the moment I must say I hardly expected to be able to accomplish anything. For, jammed between two slippery walls of ice, and only able to move my arms, cudgel my brains as I would, I could not think what was to be done. I shouted for another rope. When it came down I managed to throw one end to Thompson's left hand, which was waved about until he caught it. But, when pulled it merely dragged out of his hand. Then with some difficulty I managed to tie a noose on the rope by putting both my hands above my head. With this I lassoed that poor pathetic arm which was the only part of Thompson that could be seen. Then came the tug-of-war. If he refused to move, I could do nothing more to help him; moreover I was afraid that at any moment he might faint. If that occurred I do not believe he could have been got out at all, for the force of the fall had jammed him further down than it was possible to follow. Slowly

C. S. Thompson in the foreground and H. Kaufmann, the Swiss guide, descending from an unsuccessful first attempt on Mount Hungabee in 1901 the rope tightened, as it was cautiously pulled by those above. I could hear my heart thumping in the ghastly stillness of the place, but at last Thomson began to shift, and after some short time he was pulled into an upright position by my side. To get the rope round his body was of course hopeless. Partly by wriggling and pulling on my own rope I so shifted, that straining one arm over my head I could get my two hands together, and then tied the best and tightest jamming knot I could think of round his arm, just above the elbow. A shout to the rest of the party, and Thompson went rapidly upwards till he disappeared round the bulge of ice forty feet or more above. I can well remember the feeling of dread that came over me lest the rope should slip or his arm give way under the strain, and he should come thundering down on top of me; but he got out all right, and a moment later I followed. Most marvellously no bones had been broken, but how one could have fallen as he did without being instantaneously killed will always remain a mystery. He must have partially jammed some considerable distance higher up than the point where I found him, for he had a ruck-sack on his back, and this perhaps acted as a brake, as the walls of the crevasse closed in lower down. We were both of us nearly frozen and wet to the skin, for ice-cold water was slowly dripping the whole time on to us; and in my desire to be as little encumbered as possible, I had gone down into the crevasse very scantily clad in a flannel shirt and knicker-bockers.[8]

This dramatic incident resulted in a lifelong friendship between Collie and Thompson. Collie's letters to Thompson during the years of his Canadian explorations, from 1897 to 1913, throw interesting sidelights on some of his companions, personal opinions which are completely lacking in his published material.

After an unsuccessful attempt on Mount Balfour, Collie and Baker, who still had a few weeks of holiday left, hired an outfit and set off to the north in the direction of a high peak thought to be Mount Murchison, but which Collie subsequently discovered to be Mount Forbes, (Collie's sketch map, reproduced on page 90 shows their route.) This expedition had significant consequences. Baker started a plane table survey of the country which was completed in subsequent years by Collie and printed as the first accurate map of this region. The story of this journey is best told in Collie's letter to Thompson written shortly after his return to England:

I suppose I had better begin and roughly tell you what Baker and I did. We started from Laggan and only managed to get up the head of the Bow Valley after three days. From there we ascended a rock peak which lay due north of Aberdeen and looked down the little fork of the

Saskatchewan and the Bow Valley, not hard climbing but a good place to survey from: we then went north till we struck the Saskatchewan. You will see our route marked on the rough map in red.

From camp 7 we went up Mount Sarbach a really good rock scramble but very rotten 11,000 feet and from him located our big fellow we had seen from Mount Aberdeen. It is from Hector's map (that I have seen at Ottawa) Mount Forbes. It took us another day to get to camp 8 and the weather turned bad, snow etc. So we passed 2 days in exploring the Freshfield Glacier which is very fine and we have some good photos of it. Then we tried Forbes but were drenched to the skin and finally had to retreat in a snow storm. It is really a difficult peak a combination of the Dent Blanche and the Matterhorn. We then made tracks for the Blaeberry and found great difficulty in getting down it from camp 9-10. We also did not know where to turn south out of it to get to the Kicking Horse. So from camp 10 we climbed another rock peak and found the pass but it took us 3 days to get there for we finally had to go up one valley and cross over into another high up to do it. People have tried to get horses over it before but never got further than the pass from the south side. The weather had all this time been getting steadily worse and in the pass we were heavily snowed upon at camp 12 and for the last fortnight we were never dry. Finally we got down the North Branch which was easy and so to Field. We enjoyed ourselves muchly and I often wished you could have been with us.[9]

His imagination fired by the view of distant peaks to the north of Mount Freshfield, Collie spent the winter of 1897-98 consulting all the literature he could find that dealt with the Canadian Rockies. In a letter to Tom Wilson,* his outfitter in Banff, on March 22, 1898, Collie wrote that he had bought a work "worth its weight in gold—namely Palliser's Journals with the maps,"[10] which he and Baker were sending to Wilson. Collie noted somewhat enviously that Hector's journeys "were usually 20 or more miles a day and he climbed hills as well as provisioned the camp with sheep whilst he was doing it. We don't do such things now in the Rockies."

From Palliser's Journals Collie learned that the great peak he was in

---

* Tom Wilson, a fascinating character in his own right, came to the west from Ontario as a member of the Northwest Mounted Police but then resigned to work as a packer with the C.P.R. mountain survey. In 1882 he was the first white man to discover Lake Louise. Later he set up a packing and guiding outfit in Banff and supplied most of the early mountain explorers. A well-read man, he corresponded with Collie until his death in 1930.

search of was not Mount Murchison but Mount Forbes. He was surprised to find that much of the ground which he and Baker had travelled over the previous summer had been covered by Dr. Hector, as all the local knowledge available in 1897 dated from the C.P.R. surveys. Of the mountains around the head of the north fork of the Saskatchewan the guides in Banff appeared to know nothing. Collie was greatly intrigued by the mystery of Mount Brown and Mount Hooker. Even though Mount Brown had been dethroned to around 9000 feet, Mount Hooker had not been identified. There was always a remote possibility that David Douglas had traversed a different Athabasca Pass than the one visited by Coleman in 1893 and that the giant peaks might still exist further to the north. There was plenty of room for speculation, and every reason for hastening to Canada to achieve success and possibly fame in new geographical discoveries.

A letter from Collie reveals the rather quaint etiquette at that time whereby climbers staked out their own area of exploration and the secrecy Collie felt necessary to discourage "trespassers".

"Fay and Michael are at present trying to engage Sarbach in order to try Mount Forbes," he wrote, "I wish them luck; without Sarbach they have no chance at all. I don't know about mountaineering etiquette out in America, but over on this side of the duck pond it would have been considered the right thing to first write Baker or me to find out what we intended to do." After suggesting that Thompson attempt Mounts Murchison, Brown and a peak south of Brown which he thought to be Lyell, Collie concluded:

> All this information is private, so don't give me away by telling people of it. It is in fact what I had intended doing had I been able to come out this next summer, but as I am not, you personally are welcome to it, only if you don't do it yourself please don't tell other people and set them on at the big peaks. Especially don't give Fay (our mutual friend) any of it. If you want to have anything more, let me know and I will give you all the information I have.[11]

Although Collie had originally planned to spend the summer in the Alps, he wrote Thompson on May 4 that he had enlisted the help of two crack Alpine Club men, Hermann Woolley of Caucasian fame and another friend Hugh Stutfield:

> ... and we shall ascend or descend on the Canadian Rockies at the

end of July if all goes well. My programme is an ambitious one. Murchison from the Pipestone to begin with, then Forbes, and then we shall force our way north to Brown and Hooker by the north branch of the Saskatchewan. Could you join us for a bit at the beginning, or come the whole way if you could? We ought to have a really good time barring those damned mosquitoes—and do some really good climbing.

I hope we shan't put Fay's nose out of joint at all—but you say he is also going for Forbes—well if he hasn't a Swiss guide with him he won't do much on Forbes. Forbes is none too easy and quite a different kettle of fish from Lefroy, Victoria, or Gordon.[12]

Herman Woolley, a book publisher of independent means, had been well known in his younger days as a football player and a boxer, and for some years was amateur champion of the middleweights of the county of Lancashire. His unselfishness and imperturbable good nature were proverbial, and he himself used to attribute his successes as a pugilist to the fact that the other fellow always lost his temper first. His name appears among the early records of ascents of Pillar Rock, in the Lake District, but he did not commence regular mountaineering until his fortieth year. He then began at once to make Alpine history, and, after a brief but strenuous apprenticeship in Switzerland, he went to the Caucasus and conquered several new peaks. He had climbed in Snowdonia and in 1890 joined the large party of the Alpine Club which climbed in the Cuillin under the direction of Charles Pilkington. Like Collie, Woolley was a one-time President of the Alpine Club.

Embarking at Liverpool on July 14, Collie, now the leader of his own expedition, Stutfield*and Woolley arrived in Montreal nine days later, where they spent two nights before boarding the train for the west. On Friday July 29 they arrived in Banff, and spent a pleasant afternoon canoeing along the smooth reaches of the Bow River amidst many other boating parties. The wooded banks, the picnickers and a steam launch reminded them of the Thames at Maidenhead or Wargrave. Bill Peyto and his trail crew, Bill Byers, the cook, and Nigel Vavasour and Roy Douglas, the packers, awaited them at Laggan. There were thirteen horses, one of which subsequently broke its leg and had to be shot, and three dogs, which proved a nuisance when supplied ran short. By noon Sunday the horses were packed and they set off into the wilds. For Woolley and Stutfield the

---

*Stutfield, a keen traveller and sportsman, was the author of *El Magreb*, an account of his travels in Spain and Morocco. He climbed extensively in the Alps from 1881-1897.

In the Canadian Rockies, 1898. Collie, pipe in mouth, is nearest the teepee; Stutfield is seated on a box

experience was a new one, but their pleasure was destroyed by the hordes of mosquitoes and the half-wild Indian ponies which blundered through and over the dead timber that blocked the trail. The first few days they were tormented with terrible heat, indigestible food, and thunderstorms. An attempt to bathe in a stream was defeated by the mosquitoes and battalions of bulldog flies; refuge in a smudge of smoke made from damp grass and weeds was of little help. The third day ended in a downpour of rain which soaked everyone in camp. On Wednesday August 3 they crossed the Pipestone Pass, at 8036 feet the highest altitude to which they took the horses, and entered a grand though desolate country. Through this more open country they made good speed until they reached the lower Siffleur Valley, which was badly choked with fallen timber.

When they arrived at the Kootenay Plains on the Saskatchewan River they were impressed by the open nature of the country. The view up the valley was obscured by a fine glacier-covered mountain, which Collie named Mount Wilson after Tom Wilson of Banff. To the north the hills all but disappeared in a thick haze of copper-coloured smoke, the result, it was said, of forest fires started by thousands of wretched people trekking to the Klondike from Edmonton. The fires and the smoke at some times made them feel endangered, and at others prevented photography or map making. On Saturday, August 6, they camped beside the flooding Saskatchewan River, greatly swollen by melted ice from the sun-heated glaciers. Around the camp the talk turned to the danger of forest fires and death in the woods:

> Very tall were the yarns that circulated as the flames shot merrily upwards from the crackling logs, and the ruddy sparks flew aloft into the gloom to join company with the now dimly shining stars. Death, it was represented to us confronted the backwoods traveller in quite a remarkable variety of shapes, and even if we did not break our necks on the mountain, we gathered it would be hard times if some member of the outfit did not die of sunstroke, or drown when fording rivers. Finally, Woolley, remarking that it was getting late, announced that he was going to bed in his boots. This augmented Stutfield's already growing terror, for he slept with his head over Woolley's feet; and the latter, who was a noted footballer in his day, had a nasty way sometimes of practising place-kicks in his dreams. However, the night passed without further alarms of any sort.[13]

For the next week they slowly pushed their way upstream past the confluence of the three main branches of the Saskatchewan and, following the north fork of the river, advanced in the face of increasing difficulty towards the Sunwapta. When three horses and a foal broke away from the pack train and swam the river to an island, Peyto rescued them, but the bacon, flour, and sugar in their packs had to be spread out to dry, attracting every kind of insect life. On August 11, Colloe and Stutfield climbed Survey Peak (8781 feet), where Collie commenced the plane-table survey. When at last the grey smoke haze lifted they had a glorious view of Mount Forbes on the far side of Glacier Lake.

Travel along the west side of the north fork of the Saskatchewan was slow, for there were no trails and the men had to cut timber for three or four miles each day. On Monday August 15 Peyto and one of the packers went ahead in search of a trail, but returned dejectedly at 1 p.m. to report that further progress was impossible. "Ignoring Peyto's picturesque language, Collie remarked that the weather was exceedingly warm; they must be very thirsty; and that whisky and water wasn't a bad drink when you couldn't get any better. To this they agreed."[14] Shortly after this Peyto announced there was a chance of carrying on if only they could ford the river to the east bank. So saying he urged his mare into the water and after several plucky attempts forced a crossing. The rest of the outfit followed. On the eighteenth day a semipermanent camp was established in the woods at an elevation of 7000 feet, near the site of the present Columbia Icefield Chalet. Immediately opposite the camp to the southwest rose a noble snow-covered peak about 12,000 feet high with splendid rock cliffs and hanging glaciers; on its right the tongue of a fine glacier descended to the bottom of the valley. These they named Mount Athabasca and Athabasca Glacier, and decided to attack the peak the next day. An after-dinner inspection revealed that provisions were perilously low, due partly to the three dogs, who had devoured large amounts of bacon. There was sufficient flour for five days and bacon for two. The supplies that had been cached at the main fork of the Saskatchewan were one week's journey away. It was therefore agreed that Collie and Woolley would climb Mount Athabasca while Stutfield went in search of game.

Starting rather late on the morning of August 18, the two climbers quickly reached the small glacier on the east side of the peak. They angled upwards to the northeastern arête, a rotten limestone ridge which they soon abandoned for a glacier to the west. After working their way into the great basin underneath the summit, they again made for the northeastern

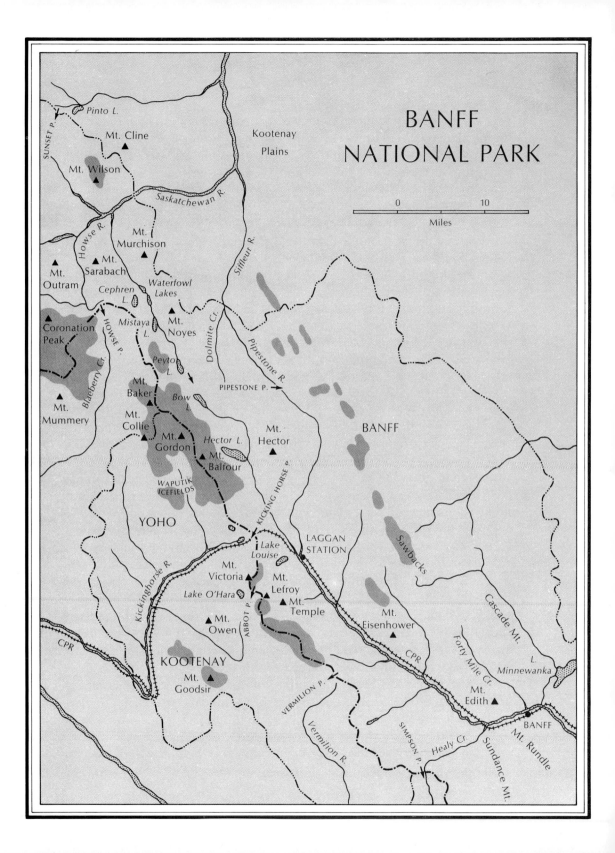

BANFF
NATIONAL PARK

Miles

0   10

Pinto L.

▲ Mt. Cline

Kootenay
Plains

▲ Mt. Wilson

SUNSET P.

Saskatchewan R.

HOWSE R.

▲ Mt.
Murchison

Siffleur R.

▲ Mt.
Sarabach

▲ Mt.
Outram

*Cephren
L.*

*Waterfowl
Lakes*

HOWSE P.

▲
Coronation
Peak

*Mistaya
L.*

▲ Mt.
Noyes

Dolmite Cr.

PIPESTONE P.

Pipestone R.

BANFF

Blaeberry Cr.

*Peyto
L.*

▲ Mt.
Mummery

▲ Mt.
Baker

*Bow
L.*

▲ Mt.
Collie

▲ Mt.
Gordon

Hector L.

▲ Mt.
Hector

▲ Mt.
Balfour

*WAPUTIK
ICEFIELDS*

YOHO

Kicking Horse R.

Kickinghorse R.

*Lake
Louise*

LAGGAN
STATION

Sawbacks

Mt.
Victoria ▲

Lake O'Hara

Mt.
Lefroy ▲

▲ Mt.
Temple

ABBOT P.

▲ Mt.
Owen

▲ Mt.
Eisenhower

Cascade Mt.

Forty Mile Cr.

CPR

KOOTENAY

▲ Mt.
Goodsir

CPR

*L.
Minnewanka*

Mt.
Edith ▲

VERMILION P.

Vermilion R.

SIMPSON P.

Healy Cr.

BANFF

Mt. Rundle

Sundance Mt.

ridge. There they were faced with a narrow and steep ice arête. Soon, Woolley, who was in the lead, was forced to cut steps in the ice. Two hours later they finally arrived at a small platform underneath the summit, only to discover a wall of perpendicular rock. Skirting the rocks to the right, they came upon a narrow chimney which led them not to the summit but to an overhanging rock fifteen feet high. Undaunted, they somehow scrambled up it and onto the summit:

> The view that lay before us in the evening light was one that does not often fall to the lot of modern mountaineers. A new world was spread at our feet; to the westward stretched a vast ice-field probably never before seen by human eye, and surrounded by entirely unknown, unnamed, and unclimbed peaks. From its vast expanse of snows the Saskatchewan glacier takes its rise, and it also supplies the headwaters of the Athabasca; while far away to the west, bending over in those unknown valleys glowing with evening light, the level snows stretched, to finally melt and flow down more than one channel into the Columbia River, and thence to the Pacific Ocean. Beyond the Saskatchewan glacier to the south-east, a high peak (which we have named Mount Saskatchewan) lay between this glacier and the west branch of the North Fork, flat-topped and covered with snow, on its eastern face a precipitous wall of rock. Mount Lyell and Mount Forbes could be seen far off in the haze. But it was towards the west and north-west that the chief interest lay. From this great snowfield rose solemnly, like "lonely seastacks in mid-ocean," two magnificent peaks, which we imagined to be 13,000 or 14,000 feet high, keeping guard over those unknown western fields of ice. One of these which reminded us of the Finsteraarhorn, we have ventured to name after the Right Hon. James Bryce, the then President of the Alpine Club. A little to the north of this peak, and directly to the westward of Peak Athabasca, rose probably the highest summit in this region of the Rocky Mountains [Mount Columbia]. Chisel-shaped at the head, covered with glaciers and snow, it stood alone, and I at once recognised the great peak I was in search of; moreover, a short distance to the north-east of this mountain, another, almost as high, also flattopped, but ringed around with sheer precipices, reared its head into the sky above its fellows.[15]

Collie and Woolley had established for the first time the presence of the Columbia Ice Field, centre of the greatest accumulation of ice in the Rocky Mountains. With its outlet glaciers, the Columbia Ice Field covers an area of nearly 150 square miles of which at least 50 square miles are more than 8500 feet above sea level. This great ice reservoir lies astride the Continental Divide for a distance of about 20 miles, and from it radiate three valleys. Melt waters flow into the three great rivers mentioned by Collie: the Athabasca (765 miles), a subtributary of the Mackenzie River which flows into the Arctic Ocean; the Saskatchewan (1205 miles) which crosses the prairies and finally empties into the Hudson Bay; and the Columbia (1210 miles) which cuts its way through mighty gorges and crosses into the United States before entering the Pacific Ocean.

Collie had mistakenly identified the two peaks as Brown and Hooker, and had overestimated their altitudes, but these were all errors that could be corrected at a later date. There was every reason to celebrate back at camp, especially as Stutfield and Vavasour had been successful in the hunt, killing three bighorn sheep to provide much needed meat. Stutfield had climbed behind the camp into a bleak upland pass first traversed by Wilcox in 1896. In honour of the early traveller Collie named it Wilcox Pass and the adjacent peak Mount Wilcox. This pass today provides a pleasant upland walk for the hiker willing to ascend behind the Chalet. Mount Wilcox, an easy peak to climb, provides a spectacular view over the Sunwapta Valley to Mount Athabasca, the Snow Dome, and some of the outlying tongues of the Columbia Ice Field.

Setting out to explore the newly discovered ice field and if possible climb one of the spectacular new peaks, Collie, Stutfield and Woolley (on Friday August 19) ascended the right bank of the Athabasca Glacier, bivouacking as high up as possible. At 1:30 a.m. after a few hours of fitful sleep, they set off by lantern light up the glacier, with a thunderstorm grumbling over the peaks to the north. The Athabasca Glacier rose in three distinct ice falls, the highest being the most crevassed. With difficulty they wound their way through the maze of towering séracs and threatening crevasses, but five hours after leaving the bivouac they stepped out onto the upper glacier. They stood on the edge of an immense ice field, stretching away mile upon mile like a rolling snow-covered prairie. The peaks, rising here and there like rocky islands in a frozen sea, were all a long way off. Mount Bryce to the southwest sent its three peaks high in the air, and north of it lay Mount Columbia, their immediate goal. Further north a double-headed mountain hid the high rock peak (afterwards named Mount Alberta), which Collie had thought might be Mount Brown. The thunder in the air became increasingly threatening as the day progressed.

A little after noon, when Mount Columbia seemed to be no nearer, they stopped to admire the vast cirque formed by Mount Columbia and the Twins, two fine peaks, one rocky, the other snow-covered, before heading back to camp. On the return journey they climbed the Snow Dome (11,340 feet), a hot and tiring ascent because the melting snow gave way at each footstep. Towards evening the thunder clouds chased them back to camp in driving rain. This long and exhausting day had established the immensity of the ice field, and confirmed that what Collie had originally thought were Brown and Hooker were in reality Mount Columbia and Mount Alberta. Observations taken from Mount Wilcox and other vantage points during the next two days of rest in camp did not suggest that there was any readily accessible path to the north where the supposed Brown and Hooker might lie.

On Wednesday August 24, Roy Douglas was left behind with half the horses while the rest moved on over Wilcox Pass. After a few miles of easy going, the trail descended into Tangle Creek, which was so steep in places that the horses slid down on their haunches. When free of this nightmare of treacherous slopes and dense undergrowth the party found themselves on the broad gravel-strewn flats of the Sunwapta River. On the lookout for a route westward into the mountains, they came, at the end of a long day's march, to the mouth of a gorge down which a good-sized creek tumbled in a picturesque cascade. The men spent the next morning panning the creek for gold but without much success. At this point they had reached mile eighty-five of the present-day Banff-Jasper Highway, but had actually covered a much greater distance. In the afternoon they made preparations to move upstream towards a group of three peaks Collie had earlier named Mount Stutfield, Mount Woolley, and the northernmost, Diadem Peak. The suggestion that a horse might be used to transport supplies up the creek provoked such strong language from Peyto that the idea was promptly abandoned. Instead Peyto had his men carry the supplies.

Bivouacking for the night at the foot of Diadem Glacier, they were awakened next morning by the patter of rain. Despite the unpromising weather, the climbers decided to tackle Mount Woolley by way of the steep glacier between it and Diadem. Just as they reached the foot of an imposing icefall which would take them onto the glacier, the thunderclouds burst and forced them to seek shelter. In five minutes the rain had stopped; "but the brief delay," Collie reported, "was probably our salvation. We were just putting on the rope to ascend the icefall, when, with a roar and a clatter, some tons of ice that had broken off near the summit came tumbling down, splintering into fragments in their descent."[16].

Collie and his friends, heeding this warning from Mount Woolley, redirected their efforts to Diadem Peak.

At first we had to make our way up slopes of loose shale and ice, and we kept fairly near the arête to avoid falling stones. This involved us in a scramble up some rather diverting rock chimneys; after which a sort of miniature rock-rib gave us safety from stones, and we followed it up to the summit. The rocks were very steep in places, and as usual, terribly insecure and splintered, and one had to be very careful. The 'diadem' of snow proved to be about a hundred feet high, set on the nearly flat top of the rocks. From the summit a wonderful panorama burst upon us, in spite of the murky atmosphere. Standing as we were near the Great Divide, we looked down on a marvellous complexity of peak and glacier, of low-lying valley, shaggy forest, and shining stream, with here and there a blue lake nestling in the recesses of the hills. Quite close, as it seemed, the overpowering mass of the supposed Mount Brown (Alberta), towered frowning many hundreds of feet above us. It is a superb peak, like a gigantic castle in shape, with terrific black cliffs falling sheer on three sides. A great wall of dark thunder-cloud loomed up over its summit; and there was a sublime aloofness, an air of grim inaccessibility, about it that was most impressive. To the west we could dimly discern the outline of another peak, with a large grey cloud floating like a canopy over it. Northwards the mountains were all much lower, and it was evident that the Columbia group formed the culmination of, at any rate, this region of the Rockies. In these northern districts the landscape, as was to be expected, presented a sterner and more forbidding aspect: indeed, the softer and more homely features of Alpine scenery were everywhere absent from these higher valleys of the western Athabasca. One missed the tiny green pastures dotted about with brown chalets, the terraced cornfields and vineyards; and the familiar tinkle of the cowbells would have sounded more musical than ever in our ears, for, as Mr. Leslie Stephen observes in "The Playground of Europe", these evidences tend to improve rather than spoil mountain scenery.[17]

Collie's companions fought off the bitter cold as best they could while he mapped the area below them. As they began the descent, the storm which had threatened all day broke around them. Pursued by driving sleet and hail, the thunder and lightning rattling and leaping around them, they hastened down the mountain by the easiest route. In the woods they were again bombarded by hailstones, and even the comfort of a dry tent was denied them. There were more thunderstorms during the night, and the next morning they retreated from these "inhospitable wilds" to their base camp on the other side of Wilcox Pass.

Roy Douglas was glad to see them return, but the celebrations were short-lived because of the food shortage. The hunting parties sent out, as far as the Brazeau River were unsuccessful; so they hurried on to the cache of supplies at the forks of the Saskatchewan. On one day they were reduced to one sardine, two anchovies and some biltong or dried meat, "which we sucked when very hungry. It is very sustaining but highly indigestible, and in appearance the reverse of appetizing. When the first morsel was put on a plate we thought that that mad wag, Byers was serving the outfit with the uppers of Peyto's boots which had recently shown signs of disintegration."[18] The semistarvation was ended when they regained the cached supplies, for in spite of their fears of theft, the bacon, flour, and whisky were intact.

After two days of feasting they carried on, spurred by the colder weather. An attempt on Mount Murchison on Friday, September 2, was defeated at an altitude of 9000 feet by heavy snow and mist. At that altitude they discovered a peculiar fossil resembling the petrified stems of pine trees broken off about a foot above the ground, with numerous fossilized remains around their base. It was later suggested that these were not trees at all, but the remains of some gigantic prehistoric seaweed. The next day, still in bad weather, they pushed on up the Mistaya River, crossed the Bow Pass and on September 5, camped on the shores of Upper Bow Lake. Early the next morning, the weather being brilliantly clear with all the forest fires extinguished by the recent rain, Collie, Stutfield and Woolley set out on the last climb of the trip. Following the north shore of Bow Lake they ascended a peak (10,119 feet), lying just to the north of the summit of the Bow Glacier's big icefall. The peak named after Collie's friend Thompson, was covered with fresh snow. From its summit they had a magnificent view of the main range of the Canadian Rockies—Mounts Assiniboine, Temple, Freshfield, Forbes and Lyell— a fitting climax to their expedition.

On September 10 the tattered band, black as chimney sweeps after their long battle with burnt timber, arrived at Laggan in time for the 5 p.m. train. With the sadness that was always present when the good fellowship of a backwoods trip was ended, they went their separate ways; Collie to England; Woolley to Vancouver and a tour of the Pacific; and Stutfield to explore the Selkirks. It had been a memorable summer with the ascent of three major peaks, Mount Athabasca, Diadem Peak, and the Snow Dome, and several lesser ones. The discovery of the Columbia Ice Fields alone justified the expedition, and throughout Collie had continued the plane-table survey first started by Baker. In forty-one days, they had covered about three hundred and twenty miles of country where trails were almost nonexistent. Mount Brown and Mount Hooker had been dethroned and replaced by Mount Columbia and Mount Alberta. No attempt had been made on Mount Forbes, and the attempt on Mount Murchison had failed. There still remained plenty of country to be explored and many mountains to be climbed.

Chapter Seven
The Canadian Rockies
1900-1902

The Canadian Rockies
1900-1902

In 1899 Collie took a well-earned rest from the Rockies, and climbed in the Alps with Major Bruce. When he wrote to Thompson on November 23, 1899, he was uncertain about returning to Canada. The uncertainty did not last long. By the end of January 1900 he was planning an expedition which would try a new approach, along the valley of the Columbia River, to the western peaks of the Columbia group. In particular he wanted to climb Mount Bryce and Mount Alberta, and to explore the "deep mysterious canyons" lying between the main chain of the Rockies and the Columbia River. Collie's inquiries in Banff in 1898 had revealed extraordinary ignorance concerning a trail down the Columbia Valley. The advent of the railway had brought a flurry of exploration by the surveyors and construction crews, and another burst of activity followed the discovery of gold at the Big Bend, but now the upper Columbia Valley was seldom visited except by prospectors and trappers. Bits of information from Tom Wilson and a prospector decided Collie in favour of a trek up the Bush River. The western approach, where heavy rainfall resulted in deeper rivers, more formidable muskeg, and denser timber, would be much more difficult than the eastern side. Another part of Collie's plan was to link up with Thompson, who would be approaching from the east.

On Sunday July 29, 1900, Collie, Stutfield and Sydney Spencer, a longtime climbing friend from Bath, alighted from the number one westbound C.P.R. train at Donald Station. Bill Peyto was away at the Boer war and his place was taken by Fred Stephens, "one of the best fellows it has ever been our good fortune to meet." Stephens, as his fellow guide Jimmy Simpson recalled him, was

a big strapping specimen from the lumber woods in Michigan, an expert woodsman and strong as a bull, but no diplomat. As soon as he got to camp he would take off his boots and socks, grab his axe, which he would take to bed with him, and go out cutting wood in his bare feet. If he stepped on a piece of juniper he would murmur something uncomplimentary, lift the foot, brush off the thorns and leave the points still in the skin and go on with his chopping. No wonder Collie liked him; we all did.[1]

He was Collie's guide on the next three trips, and a lifelong friendship sprang up, carried on by the twice yearly exchange of letters over the next twenty-five years.

Troubles plagued the expedition from the start. As the expert axeman was trying to mount one of the new pinto ponies, it rolled over on him, nearly killing him. The replacement hurriedly wired for proved unequal to the task imposed upon him by the miles of fallen timber and tangled bush the party encountered. The first thirty-six miles along the Columbia Valley, despite the luxuriant growth, were covered with little difficulty. On Friday August 3 they arrived on the south bank of the Bush River, and their ordeal began. Beset by mosquitoes swarming in the damp vegetation, the men spent two days hacking out a one mile trail over a rocky spur and carrying their supplies to the summit of the spur, too steep for laden ponies. Rain set in, and continued intermittently for the rest of the journey. For the next week, they laboured up the south bank of the Bush River. Collie, who for three days took a turn with the axe, described the wet forest in his notebook:

> We forced our way into the woods where the piled refuse of years of decay and disaster lay rotting in the wet dense undergrowth. The chopping of the axe and the drip of the water from the leaves are the only sounds, unless unprintable language is suddenly hurled at some wretched pack animal that straying from the others tries to find a few scant leaves of wet grass away from the trail: weary wetness. Sopped to the waist wading streams of ice cold water, or drenched by the leaves of the trees that shower down great drops of water whenever they are touched or the breeze shakes them.[2]

Much to their relief they finally camped in a pleasant site on the north bank of the Bush, half a mile below the junction of its forks. Above them towered the great peak they believed to be Mount Bryce. The camp, 2800 feet by the mercury barometer, was only slightly higher than Donald Station, which they had left eighteen days earlier. Collie now suspected that they might not have advanced far enough into the mountains to be close to the great ice fields, which on the eastern approaches to the Rockies were about 5000 to 7000 feet. While investigating the south fork on August 19, Collie and Stutfield reached an upper woodland from which they could see at the head of the valley, about twenty-five miles away, a beautiful snow pyramid rising from an immense ice field. Without doubt this was Mount Columbia, but far removed from its expected position. Collie concluded that the maps they had been using were faulty. Puzzled and disheartened, they returned through the "hateful" woods to the tethered horses and thence to the camp.

Before plunging onward Collie and Spencer climbed the peak in the angle of the forks which they thought to be Mount Bryce. The struggle was intense and fought through thick bush for over 5000 feet. Fortunately the day was fine and the view from the summit showed a remarkable panorama of the main Rocky Mountain range. Ten miles or more northward up the north fork was Mount Bryce, and beyond that Mount Columbia rising out of the great ice field that Collie had explored in 1898. They were about twelve miles south of where they had thought themselves to be. The Columbia Ice Field, their principal goal, lay fifteen miles up a valley of dense bush, every yard of which would have to be hacked out with an axe.

After making a cache of excess supplies and baggage, they travelled up the north fork on August 21, determined to reach as far into the mountains as possible. Within an hour or two, they were forced by the impassable scaffolding of fallen timber to head the horses straight up the hill to their right. In torrents of rain they worked up more than 4000 feet of steep, heavily wooded mountainside close to Goat Peak, as they had named the false Mount Bryce. Camp was established at tree line, about 7300 feet, where the only source of drinking water was snow fetched from several hundred yards away. Stutfield hunted goat and returned with fresh meat which was a welcome change from bacon and tinned meat. They spent a week in this high camp waiting for the weather to clear, but frequent blizzards, rain and cold wind prevented any advance. Reluctant to give up the expedition without at least one good climb, Collie, Stutfield, Spencer and Stephens attempted a bold rock peak to the west, nearly 11,000 feet high. They followed a ridge beyond Goat Peak, advancing for more than an hour up a good-sized glacier, before the clouds rolled in, forcing them to return to camp.

The return down the Bush River was easier as the floods had subsided and the trail had been cut. After a journey of thirty-six days which had covered a distance of less than one hundred miles, they finally arrived back at Donald Station in pouring rain. Although Collie's disappointment was great, he had nevertheless completed a survey of the western slopes of the Rockies under appalling conditions, and discovered the formidable obstacles to be overcome in any approach to the mountains from that side. He had also failed to meet up with his friend Thompson who had been exploring in the region of the Alexandra River. From a pass between Mount Bryce and Watchman Peak the American climber looked down on the western slopes of the Rockies where far to the south Collie was fighting his way up the Bush River. It was the closest they came to each other that year.

While Collie was climbing in Norway in 1901, professional European teams, among them those of Edward Whymper, conqueror of the Matterhorn, and Dr. Jean Habel, a noted German climber-explorer, were making systematic assaults on the peaks of the Canadian Rockies. Such activity called down Collie's wrath, for reasons explained in the following letter to Thompson, dated March 21, 1901.

> I doubt whether you have heard that the great Whymper is about to attack the Rockies during 1901-2-3. He has got the two finest Swiss guides, Klucker and Pollinger, and two others and will go to Banff and then polish off all the peaks. I am dreadfully sorry for it will all be done for advertisement. Why the devil he couldn't leave them alone I don't know. He will simply go and gobble up the whole lot.
>
> As a hunting ground for amateurs the country was big enough and to spare, but when a professional team lets itself loose—well all I can say is *damn* the man! I certainly can't get over there next summer, but if I could I would try my level best to spoil some of his game for him.
>
> Why I am so mad about it is that it is not done for sport at all or because Whymper has any real liking for the hills. From the beginning it is dollars and I only wish the Appalachian Club, who pioneered all the climbing there, would go there in force next summer.[3]

During the summer of 1901 the Rev. James Outram, an extraordinarily energetic climber, made an ascent of Mount Chancellor with G.M. Weed, J. H. Scattergood and a Swiss guide, an adventure which fired his ambitions for further exploration and climbing. That following winter he broached the idea of joining forces to Collie. What Collie thought of the matter may be gathered from a letter to Thompson dated March 13, 1902.

> We must try to get together to circumvent that interloper Outram; it is a shame that you, Wilcox etc. should do all the pioneer work and then have all the cream skimmed off by a man who has had all the hard work done for him, not to mention the assistance of the Swiss guides. There is no use shutting one's eyes to the fact that professional guides are an

enormous help and on difficult mountains enable one to make much better time and get over difficulties more easily. Therefore I hope that you have managed to engage Kaufmann for the ensuing season.[4]

Thompson had indeed engaged Kaufmann, and Collie, Woolley and Stutfield reached Laggan on July 19, 1902. They hoped to climb virgin summits (while there were still a few left), to clear up some geographical uncertainties resulting from their previous journeys, when they had mapped about 3000 square miles, and to establish the altitude of some of the highest peaks. The main target was Mount Forbes, which Collie had always considered a difficult mountain. From its summit he hoped to survey the Lyell Ice Field or look for an easy pass across the watershed between Mount Forbes and the Freshfield group. To try to circumvent the food shortage which had plagued them during three seasons in the Rockies, Collie had asked Fred Stephens to double the estimate of supplies for a seven- to eight-week period, and to take half the food to a cache on the forks of the Saskatchewan. Even with this precaution there were few provisions left at the end of the expedition.

At Laggan, the British climbers were met by Thompson, Weed and the Swiss guide Hans Kaufmann, as well as Fred Stephens and the packer Robson. Thompson, however, was immediately recalled by a telegram

The various peaks of Mount Murchison from Mount Noyes, August, 1902

announcing that his house in Texas had been burned down. The first night in the Rockies was spent sorting baggage in the railway station. The luggage, "owing to our fixed determination to make ourselves comfortable, was somewhat bulkier than usual," noted Collie. "One depraved person, for instance, had brought a camp-bedstead. This luxury was viewed with the strongest disapproval, as out West, for some occult reason, it is considered unmanly to sleep otherwise than on the ground. Weed, hardy man, had neither cork mattress nor bedstead; but, like a true son of America, lay in his blanket and a ground sheet."[5]

The next day they moved out, joining the other two packers, Clarence Murray and Dave Tewksbury, a lumberman from Wisconsin. Everything seemed so entirely different from the miserable journey up the Bush River. The trail up Bow River was now well travelled and kept free of deadfall. The weather was fine and even the mosquitoes were less ferocious. On the afternoon of Monday, July 28, the party arrived at the campsite beside the Saskatchewan River. After inspecting the river, which was unusually high, Collie went in search of two bottles, one of whisky, the other of brandy, which he had buried at the foot of a tree in 1898. The ground was well dug over, as many a thirsty trapper, prospector and trailhand had searched for these bottles, but without success. Collie located the burial place without difficulty, for he had an excellent memory for detail, and copious libations were drunk that night around the campfire. Outram's party, they discovered from a note at their supply cabin, would meet them at the foot of Mount Forbes. While waiting for the river to recede, Collie, Stutfield, Weed and Kaufmann made the first ascent of Mount Murchison (10,936 feet) by following a route slightly north of Collie's 1898 attempt.

A few days later they joined Outram's party and established a base camp at the junction of the Forbes and Freshfield brooks. Outram, flushed with triumph from making the first ascent of Mount Lyell and Mount Columbia, must have grated on Collie's nerves.

The combined climbing teams set out at daybreak on August 4 for Mount Freshfield (10,945 feet). Their route, similar to that taken by Collie, Baker and Sarbach in 1897, took them diagonally up a steep snow-slope onto the glacier. After halting for a late breakfast on the eastern arête, where the 1897 party had been forced to turn back, the climbers continued on two ropes, one of Collie, Stutfield, Woolley and Hans Kaufmann and the other of Outram, Weed and Hans' brother Christian, Outram's guide.

For some distance above the breakfast-place the climbing was easy enough and we began to fancy we might reach the summit without serious difficulty. Higher up, however, the arête was broken by several formidable gendarmes, or buttresses of crag, with some pretty difficult rock-faces, which gave a good deal of trouble. At first we thought of traversing below on the left; but the rocks were too steep and insecure to render the operation a safe one, even supposing it had been practicable. In the end we kept to the crest of the arête the whole way, Hans negotiating the bad places with much skill. As usual, the chief difficulty consisted in the abominably rotten and splintered character of the rock; but one or two narrow cracks, or chimneys, served us in good stead, and foot by foot we gradually made our way till we suddenly found ourselves on the snow cornice within a few yards of the summit.[6]

The prospect from the top Collie described as one of the finest in the Canadian Rockies. From Freshfield, which lies between the Laggan and Waputik groups and the Lyell and Columbia Ice Fields, Bush Peak and the scene of Collie's labours two years earlier seemed quite close. To the north were the mountains he had explored in 1898 including Columbia, Athabasca, Alberta, the Twins, the Snow Dome and Saskatchewan. But close at hand was Mount Forbes the chief objective of their expedition.

Much nearer, and quite free from cloud, by far the most commanding feature on view, was the stately pyramid of Forbes; and we scanned for the first time, and with critical eyes, the western side of the arête by which we hoped to climb it. It was not particularly gratifying to find that the notch looked even worse from this side than from the other, as the cliffs immediately underneath fell perfectly sheer; and there was evidently no chance whatever of our being able to traverse below on either side. A brief comparison with the height of our own peak was enough to show that Forbes would have to come down in the world at least as much as Freshfield.[7]

As well as being a first ascent of a high and difficult peak, this climb was important because it enabled Collie to link up his survey on the eastern side of the main Rocky Mountain chain with his survey on the western side. In addition he discovered a new pass over the mountains, the Bush Pass, which he explored a few days later. Although not a very practical route because of the difficulties of the Bush River valley, it was the only pass between Thompson to the north and Howse to the south.

The climbers rested for a few days while the trail crew cut a trail to the base of Mount Forbes and set up an advanced base camp in a small clearing denuded of trees by an avalanche many years before. On the afternoon of Saturday August 9, after a substantial lunch, the climbers shouldered their packs and one by one made their way up the steep wooded hillside. They bivouacked at a minature alp, carpeted with a profusion of flowers and watered by a gurgling brook. The day being Coronation Day, they drank their Majesties' health with tea and well-watered whisky, and as a further momento of the occasion named a fine snow-clad peak to the south, Coronation Peak.

Collie, Woolley and Outram each published a description of the next day's climb. Collie's, which is given below, is the most concise but as always he minimizes the dangers; not because he ignored them, but because he disliked overdramatizing any particular situation. Mount Forbes was the most difficult and dangerous climb that he undertook in Canada, as his letters to Thompson make clear. The greatest danger was from the loose, rotten rocks which made every hold unreliable. The shortage of climbing rope, sixty feet for one party and eighty feet for the other, greatly interfered with the safety and the speed of the climb, as Collie, who at one point unroped himself, was well aware.

It was still quite dark when the guides, in orthodox Alpine fashion, aroused us from our lairs, and at 5 o'clock (4 a.m. by British Columbia time) we were off. The weather was perfect, with a light but cool breeze blowing. Grass and shale-slopes, easy rocks, and a tramp up a small snow-covered glacier brought us to the arête; and from this point the climbing was pretty stiff and continuous. The rocks, which had looked

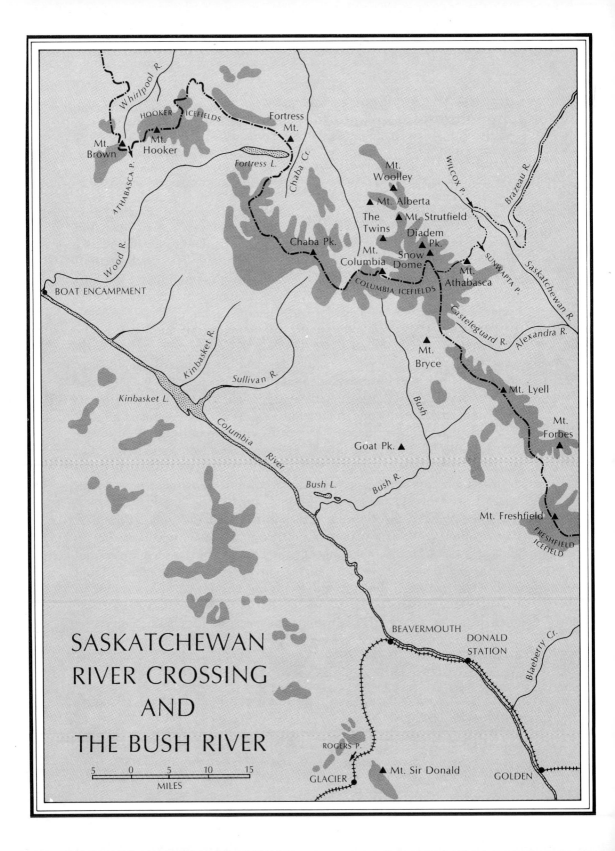

Whirlpool R.

HOOKER ICEFIELDS

Fortress Mt.

Mt. Brown

Mt. Hooker

Fortress L.

ATHABASCA P.

Chaba Cr.

Mt. Woolley

Mt. Alberta

WILCOX P.

Brazeau R.

Wood R.

The Twins

Mt. Strutfield

Chaba Pk.

Diadem Pk.

Mt. Columbia

Snow Dome

SUNWAPTA P.

Saskatchewan R.

Mt. Athabasca

COLUMBIA ICEFIELDS

BOAT ENCAMPMENT

Kinbasket R.

Sullivan R.

Castleguard R.

Alexandra R.

Kinbasket L.

Mt. Bryce

Columbia River

Bush

Mt. Lyell

Mt. Forbes

Goat Pk.

Bush L.

Bush R.

Mt. Freshfield

FRESHFIELD ICEFIELD

BEAVERMOUTH

DONALD STATION

Blaeberry Cr.

SASKATCHEWAN RIVER CROSSING AND THE BUSH RIVER

ROGERS P.

Mt. Sir Donald

GLACIER

GOLDEN

5   0   5   10   15
MILES

easy enough from below, proved to be no child's play, being a good deal steeper than we had anticipated, and very deficient in hand-hold or foothold: indeed, one or two pitches, forty or fifty feet high were distinctly difficult. On our right the face of the mountain was hollowed out into a large corrie, with sides of brown scaly rock suggestive of rhinoceros hide, that were most unprepossessing: in fact, it must be admitted that Forbes is much more beautiful at a distance than when you are actually standing upon him.

Owing to the steepness of the rocks some hours elapsed before a convenient breakfast-place presented itself; and by the time we found one we were all pretty hungry. Above the breakfasting-place we left the arête and skirted a short distance to the right, arriving on the summit of the miniature Pic Tyndall soon after half-past ten. From here we dropped down into the dreaded notch, and the gymnase, or sensational part of the climb, began. Beyond the notch was a smooth upright buttress that was decidedly formidable, and the arête contracted to a narrow knife-edge of rock set at a very steep angle. Very slowly, inch by inch, we edged our way upwards—now à cheval, astride of the uncomfortably sharp crest of the ridge, now clinging like limpets to the rocks at the side, for there was very little to catch hold of. On the left the cliffs fell perfectly sheer for some hundreds of feet, with mingled snow and rock declivities fifteen hundred feet or so below: on the right was the great precipice of the eastern face. The climb at this point resembled that on the Zinal side of the Rothhorn more than anything else with which we are acquainted; but the rocks were not nearly so good . . .

Towards the top the rocks became most extraordinarily rotten, alternating with intervals of snow cornice. To quote from Woolley's paper in the *Alpine Journal*: "The narrow crest of the ridge seemed to be held together only by the snow frozen against its sides, and in case of the snow melting it appeared that the first westerly gale might easily hurl the whole structure down the great eastern precipice, on its way to augment the shingle-flats of the Middle Fork. In places the piled-up snow certainly favoured us by bridging over spaces where the loose rocks, if bare, would have been a source of danger". At one part the sensation was as if we were walking along the top of a very ill-constructed Scotch dyke—only with a big precipice below on either side—although, doubtless, having withstood the buffeting of the tempests that beat upon the peak, there was little fear of its proving unequal to supporting our puny weight. A straddle along a most insecure-looking edge of wind-drifted snow—a very chilly and uncomfortable sort of saddle—was the last of our acrobatic performances; and a short snow-slope terminating in a cornice overhanging the eastern escarpment led us, soon after two o'clock, to the little snowcap that forms the summit.[8]

Collie makes light of the "very ill-constructed Scotch dyke" near the summit. Outram, who had a greater sense of the dramatic, considered it a very dangerous place indeed. When Weed was crossing the worst part, a huge mass of rock tumbled off the ridge and thundered down the western precipice. This served to clear most of the debris so that the others crossed in relative safety.

A piercing cold wind had sprung up during the ascent, limiting their stay on the summit. To the south a tall column of smoke rose from the forest of the Columbia Valley; the smoke was to interfere with the views and photographs for many days to come. After thirty minutes they began the descent, leaving behind a small Union Jack. This time the whole party was roped together as they went down the snow slopes on the northwestern side. Christian Kaufmann cut steps in the steep ice for over 1500 feet. Then they were able to kick steps in softer snow to reach a small col which connected Forbes with the mountains on the west. When Collie looked at this ice face ten days later, from the Lyell Glacier, he noted that much of the ice and snow had avalanched from the heat of summer. Finally, by skirting underneath the western precipices, they reached the foot of the southern ridge of Forbes, where their climb had started.

Outram's party having withdrawn, Collie and his companions made an uneventful first ascent of Howse Peak (10,793 feet) on August 14, and then moved camp to the east end of Glacier Lake. Prevented from taking the horses along the north shore of the lake to the Lyell Glacier by a smouldering forest fire, believed to have been started by Outram's party, they spent a rainy Sunday in the varied and interesting conversation so dear to Collie's heart. Robson, who had fought through the Boer War with Strathcona's Horse, had a great dislike of those who did not know the peculiarities of horses or of survival on the open veldt. Fred Stephens told of his trapping and hunting adventures, mostly in his home state of Michigan; Dave Tewksbury discussed the rugged life in the lumber camps of the far west, where the work was hard, the pay poor, but the food was good; Clarence Murray talked of farming. Hans Kaufmann, whose knowledge of English was limited, contentedly listened. And what tales Collie must have told these sturdy frontiersmen of his adventures in Scotland, Switzerland, Norway and the Himalaya!

As the heavy rain had not extinguished the forest fire, Stephens and Tewksbury spent two days building a raft with a platform to raise the passengers and cargo clear of any splashing waves. On a brilliant morning, without a breath of wind, the three-ton "Glacier Belle," floated off on her maiden voyage. A voyage of a few hours took them to the western end of the lake, where low lying swampy ground forced them up onto a hillside to camp in the forest. For two days they explored the Lyell Glacier, probably following Dr. Hector's trail of 1858. To the utter dismay of Hans Kaufmann, they did not climb Mount Lyell because of bad weather, but contented themselves with scrambling up a small snow-covered hill to survey the rest of the glacier. On the way down, Collie knocked his pipe out of his mouth with the ice axe, and in attempting to save it lost his balance, rolling head over heels to the bottom of the steep slope. This was his only recorded slip while climbing.

Collie had now completed the exploration of the last of the four great plateaus of ice and snow in this region of the Canadian Rockies—the Lyell, the Columbia, the Freshfield and Waputik glaciers. The party therefore decided to hasten to Laggan, to climb in the Valley of the Ten Peaks near Lake Louise.

They recovered the horses and pushed on, camping at the forks of the Saskatchewan one night, and at the lower Waterfowl Lakes the next. Leaving the pack train on the third day, Collie, Stutfield, Weed and Woolley climbed a rocky peak which Collie named after Rev. Charles L. Noyes, who with Thompson and Weed had visited the Dolomite Creek immediately to the east in 1898. The view from the top was sufficient to tell Collie all he wanted to learn of the land to the east. There were no hidden mountains or secret valleys. Almost due north and to the right of Mount Murchison, a high mountain stood out overlooking the historic Kootenay Plain. Collie named it Mount Cline, after a trader who, in earlier times, had journeyed from this region to Jasper.

Rejoining the pack train, they crossed the Bow Pass on the last lap of the homeward journey. Here they were once more beset by hordes of bull-dog flies. Beyond Bow Lake, swarms of wasps—yellow jackets— added to the misery of the unfortunate ponies; throughout the day, one or more of them would suddenly leap in the air or gallop madly through the woods, shedding packs in all directions. The packers were kept busy, and Robson was particularly vitriolic about a large mattress, or "bedroom suite" as he preferred to call it, which spent half its time lying on the ground. On the last few miles of the trail they met three outfits heading north, a sure sign of the growing popularity of the Canadian Rockies. They arrived at Laggan on Wednesday August 27, where the tents were hardly erected before a hailstorm set in, the precursor of ten days of bad weather.

Next morning they rode along the carriage road to Lake Louise. The C.P.R., which had been busy developing this area for tourists, had constructed a trail along the shoulder of Mount Temple at timber line.

"The Glacier Belle," with Dave Tewksbury as captain, and Collie and the other climbers as crew, on Glacier Lake, August 19, 1902

Rounding a corner of the hill, they had a magnificent view of Moraine Lake surrounded by the tremendous precipices of the Ten Peaks, a view which has delighted thousands of mountain lovers to this day. They moved up the valley looking for a suitable campsite, but a violent snowstorm forced them to seek shelter in the woods opposite the centre of the Ten Peaks. The Peaks had been named after the first ten numerals of the Indian language by S.E.S. Allen and Hungabee (The Chieftan) had been included as one of the ten.

When the weather finally cleared five days later, they decided to attempt Neptuak (Peak Nine). It offered a sporting chance from a pass which Weed had crossed during an unsuccessful attempt on Hungabee the previous year, and proved to be one of the best climbs of the trip. It was good hard scrambling all the way, on rocks which were firmer than usual for the Canadian Rockies. Most of the pitches were nearly vertical, and in places the handholds were scant. With five climbers on one rope progress was slow, but eventually they reached the summit. Immediately to the north, Hungabee stood out as the highest peak in the range. Beyond stood the massive forms of Lefroy and Victoria, reminders of the epic first ascents of 1897. Across Prospectors Valley, Mount Vaux stood out, and beyond that the three lofty pinnacles of Mount Goodsir. Further to the west a sea of mountains rolled wave upon wave into the farthest distance. A half-hour was spent on the summit taking bearings and photographing, until in the lengthening shadows they climbed down the rocks and arrived back in camp after sundown. Neptuak was the last climb of 1902.

At Lake Louise Chalet they took a sorrowful farewell of Hans Kaufmann, a first-rate guide.

An occasion of still greater regret was our parting, on the cars that evening towards midnight, with Fred, who accompanied us aboard 'Number 2' on the way to his home at Lacombe. Much of the success, as well as the pleasure and good-fellowship of our expeditions in 1900 and 1902 had been due to his unfailing tact, good temper and management: and when we said goodbye to him and stepped out on the platform at Banff, we felt we were at the same time bidding farewell to the Canadian Rockies.[9]

Chapter Eight

The Lofoten Islands

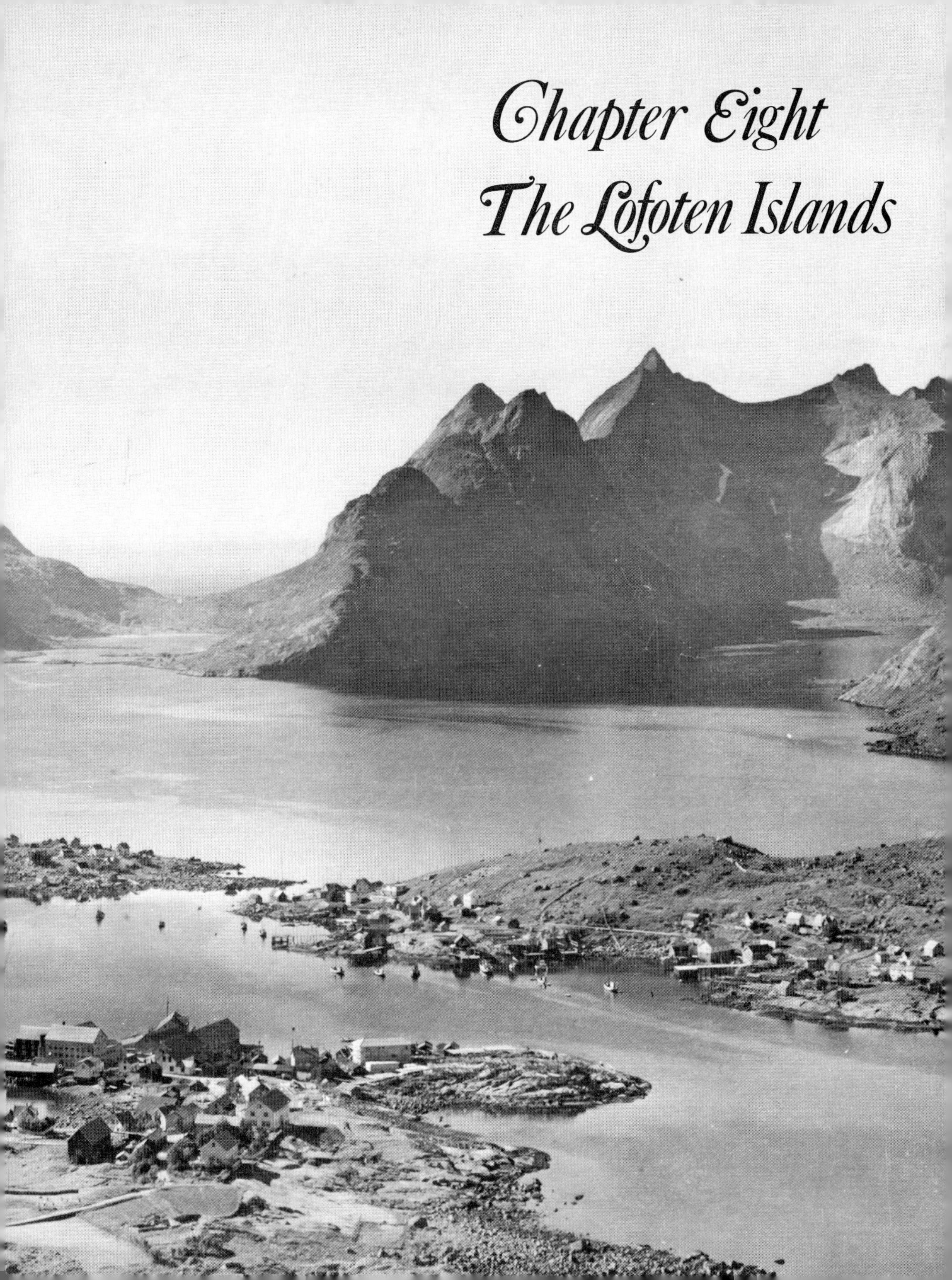

The Lofoten Islands

For many years Collie had wanted to climb the mountains of Norway. W.C. Slingsby had aroused the interest of the Alpine world in the Norwegian peaks with his exploits there, beginning with the first traverse of the Hornung group of mountains, at that time unexplored, in 1874. The year 1903, when he and Collie climbed in the Lofoten Islands, marked his fourteenth expedition to Norway. Over the years he had taken part in the first ascents of some eighteen peaks, five of them, including the highest, Skagastölstind, during a period of six days in 1876, and had pioneered new routes up mountains already conquered. Reputed to have introduced skis, indigenous to Scandinavia, to Alpine sportsmen, Slingsby must have also passed on much of his knowledge of the area, in friendly conversations as well as in his book *Norway: the Northern Playground*.

Collie made his first trip to Norway not with Slingsby, however, but with his companion from Nanga Parbat, Geoffrey Hastings. Hastings had visited the Lofoten with Hermann Woolley and L. B. Priestman in 1897, during the summer of Collie's first visit to the Canadian Rockies. These three, who knew the local conditions very well and could speak Norwegian fluently, invited Collie to join them for a short expedition in the summer of 1901. Collie at this time was forty-two years old, and the prospect of the islands must have seemed particularly inviting after his gruelling trip up the Bush River in Canada the previous summer.

The Lofoten Islands consist of two adjacent island groups extending about one hundred and fifty miles from the northeast to the southwest. They run roughly parallel to the Norwegian coast at a distance varying from one to fifty miles. Lying well within the Arctic Circle, these islands enjoy a temperate climate because of the influence of the North Atlantic Drift, that extension of the Gulf Stream, which arising in the Gulf of Mexico, sweeps thousands of miles across the Atlantic to dissipate beyond the north coast of Norway. Intense glaciation has stripped the islands of their topsoil. Heavy rain and marine abrasion have helped sharpen the features into stark slopes almost devoid of vegetation. Although in some ways they resemble the islands of Skye or the Outer Hebrides when seen from a distance, the Lofoten Islands are far wilder. The mountains are not exceptionally high, few being more than 4000 feet, but the sound rock formation, combined with steep spires and sharp ridges, make for excellent climbing. The perpetual daylight in summertime, the ease of approach, usually by sea, to the base of the peaks, the sheltered valleys for camping, and the remoteness from large numbers of tourists recommend the islands to the mountaineer in search of new adventure.

The chief islands of the Lofoten group are Rost, Vaeroy, Moskenes, Vestvagoy and Austvagoy. The famous Maelstrom, a grim whirlpool described so eloquently by Edgar Allan Poe in one of his stories, lies south of Moskenes. The other group of islands, the Vesteralens, separated from the Lofotens by a narrow sea channel, includes the islands of Hinnoy, Langoy and Andoy. Svolvaer on Austvagoy and Harstad on Hinnoy are the only towns.

Collie noted:

> The approach to the Lofoten Islands from the south after one has passed the Arctic Circle is particularly grand and beautiful. The mountains owing to the excessive prehistoric glaciation, possess forms at once curious and peculiar, giving an individuality to the view which is lacking further south on the Norwegian coast. Lofoten, however is not seen till the great West Fjord is reached, then far away across thirty miles of blue waters, which slowly pulsate with the long waves of the open sea, appears a wonderful band of sharp pointed peaks that with a deep sapphire colour outshines the deeper purple of the restless sea.[1]

The party of Collie, Hastings, Woolley and Priestman landed from the interisland steamer at Svolvaer, a harbour remarkable for its narrow approach, and for the series of rocky islands on which the town is built. On August 2, they loaded their baggage into two small boats, and rowed by local fishermen, moved to a campsite near the head of Östnes Fjord. A Norwegian who had been with Hastings on a previous occasion, came with them as a porter. One boat was left at the camp, while the fishermen returned to Svolvaer in the other. Over the next two weeks, Hastings, who enjoyed his comforts and had a gift for scrounging, visited various houses on the fjord, borrowing cooking stoves, spades, nails and poles. At the end of their stay, his tent had "assumed the appearance of a really first-class gipsy encampment." Nevertheless Hastings' spades proved their worth during the heavy rains when drainage channels had to be dug. The poles and nails were used for stringing clotheslines on which to hang their wet clothes.

The highest peak on the Lofoten Islands, Mösadlen, had been climbed, but the next three, Higraf Tind (3780 feet), Gjeitgaljar (3560 feet) and Rulten (3490 feet) had not. Opposite their campsite was the peak Gjeitgaljar, looking like a little Dru, with a ridge in front of it made up of apparently inaccessible pinnacles. The day after setting up camp, while Hastings pottered around making improvements, Collie and Woolley scrambled straight up the hillside behind the camp, climbing steep slabs of glacier-worn rock to a fine rocky ridge at 3000 feet. They were delighted with the nature of the climbing which, although nearly vertical and very exposed throughout, offered secure holds. From the ridge the surrounding peaks were clearly visible, and Collie enjoyed a pleasant hour photographing the scenery. It was fortunate that the weather should have been kind on that first day, for in the evening the heavens opened and the camp was deluged with pouring rain for the next two days. Hastings' ingenuity was extended to its utmost constructing drainage channels and dams to prevent the floods sweeping through the tents. With the return of fine weather they hung out all the bedding and spare clothes to dry before rowing the boat across a small arm of the fjord to the beach at Liland. Making their way through thickets of dwarf birch which covered the narrow valley floor, they arrived at the starting point for the first ascent of Higraf Tind.

A high ridge connecting Higraf Tind and Gjeitgaljar blocked the head of the valley in which they stood. This ridge was broken up into pinnacles and notches which appeared too precipitous for safe climbing. Turning aside from the ridge they ascended a gully to the left. This in turn led to a narrow ledge slanting upwards across the steep north face of Higraf Tind. From the ledge their route ascended vertically over slabs of rock, in and out of narrow gullies, and up slender cracks which seamed this face. After an exhilarating struggle lasting several hours, they eventually reached what appeared to be the summit.

Collie wrote:

A short distance below the top, a small promontory on the ridge afforded a splendid point from which a photograph could be taken. Woolley was sent on so that he might be photographed, proudly plant- ing his iceaxe on the topmost pinnacle. In due time he appeared against the sky; but immediately afterwards from his gesticulations I could see that something was wrong. The reason was obvious when after a few moments I joined him. Twenty feet away was another higher summit, and between the two a gulf was fixed.

Below us the rock fell sheer for over thirty feet with never a crack in it, whilst on the opposite side of the chasm the great blocks overhung, so that even had we descended hand over hand into the gap, direct ascent on the other side was hopeless.

But remembering our tactics lower down we tried further back for a traverse, and soon found that by climbing down a crack between two huge blocks on the eastern side we could get round into the gap. So far so good, but how to surmount the difficulties on the further side! An attempt to traverse on the western side was seen to be hopeless, but an obliging ledge on the other face ran round a corner. Where would it lead to? Cautiously we edged along it, passing under the summit of the mountain. Another crack between great slabs was found; up this we clambered, and once at its top all difficulty disappeared. We had conquered Higraf Tind, and all that remained for us to do was to crown the vanquished mountain with a cairn.[2]

The cairn was duly built before they descended to the first summit where their rucksacks and cameras had been left. Here they rested in the warm sunlight enjoying a late lunch and at the same time admiring the spectacular view of numberless rocky peaks around them and of the outer Lofoten Islands disappearing into the atmospheric blue of the horizon. At their feet lay the Blaaskovl Glacier and far out to sea a solitary iceberg floated by. At this time of the year when the sun never set, there was no hurry to return before dark. Reluctantly they descended to the valley and rowed back to the camp by the Östnes Fjord. That night bad weather again set in. Torrential rain fell continuously for three days and nights. An aluminum pan left outside a tent registered three inches in a three-hour period. Once again much of their time was spent digging trenches to keep their tents from washing away.

With the return of fine weather they attempted the ascent of Rulten (3490 feet), the fourth highest peak on the islands. They rowed across the fjord and landed in a small bay at the base of the mountain. Then followed a hard steep climb up ledges and gullies, made more tiresome because the day was moist and warm. Finally they emerged onto the true southwest arête, having discovered a most remarkable window in one of the ridges on the way up.   Collie wrote:

> The difficulties now began, for the ridge at once steepened; moreover, in slimness it almost resembled the Grépon. I tried to climb straight up the ridge, but perpendicular slabs, with only small cracks in them, barred the way. To be outside the mountain, when in peculiarly difficult places, is by no means pleasant. The imagination is far less troubled with ideas of what might happen should one fall, when the extreme steepness is partially hidden from one's view in the privacy of a rock chimney.[3]

Unable to make a direct ascent Collie tried edging out to the left. Perpendicular slabs of rock without holds barred the way. To the right progress was impossible because of a formidable overhang. At a height of 3000 feet, about 800 feet below the summit they turned back.

The caution revealed by Collie on this remote Norwegian peak is typical of the man, and shows a striking contrast to the approach Mummery might have used. There is little doubt that to Collie the enjoyment of mountain scenery, and the pleasures of outdoor life in remote places were all important. Collie often gives the impression in his writings that he wanted to scale a difficult peak just so that he might seek out a sheltered ledge where he could recline in comfort in a heady cloud of tobacco smoke. Even when resting Collie noticed everything. Trained to accurate observation he had an unfailing memory about the mountains he had climbed and the safe routes up them. To Mummery, however, the summit was everything, and no risk was too great in order to gain it. Mummery would gamble everything on one reckless attempt up even the most improbable route. Collie on the other hand would consider the possibilities, and then select the safest route. The failure on Rulten therefore was no great disappointment. He could still return at another time and conquer it.

During the climb on Rulten, Collie noticed that the fjord was dotted with thousands of fishing boats. Upon return to camp they found the fishermen taking advantage of the fine weather by spreading their herring nets over the rocks to dry. The climbers followed this example and tying their climbing ropes to Hastings' poles, hung up their damp bedding. While Hastings tidied up the camp, Collie and the others bathed in the clear waters of the fjord, diving in from the smoothly polished rocks on the shore.

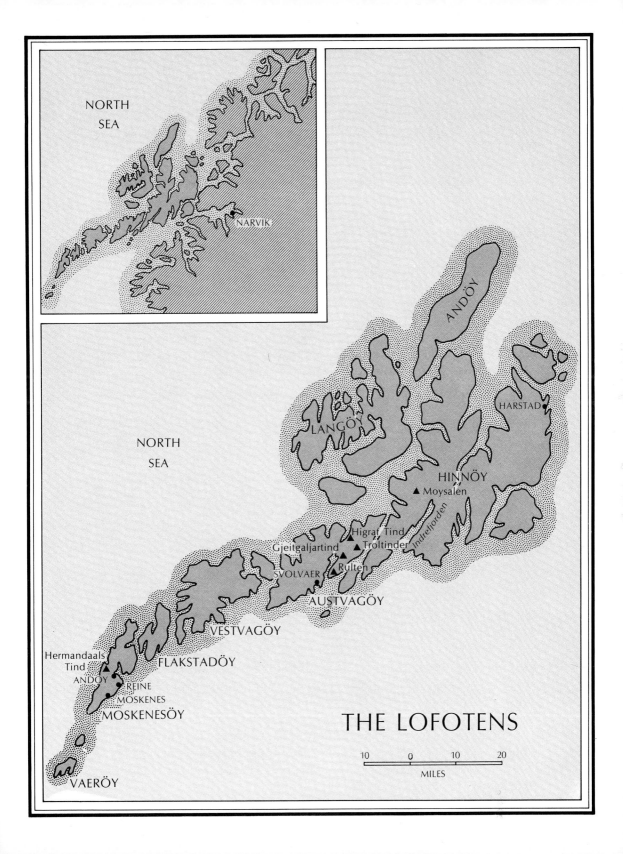

NORTH
SEA

NARVIK

NORTH

SEA

ANDÖY

HARSTAD

LANGÖY

HINNÖY

▲ Moysalen

Higraf Tind
Gjeitgaljartind   ▲ ▲ Tröltinder
                      ▲
SVOLVAER   ▲ Rulten

AUSTVAGÖY

VESTVAGÖY

Hermandaals
Tind   ▲
ANDÖY   ● REINE
          ● MOSKENES
MOSKENESÖY

Indrefjorden

FLAKSTADÖY

THE LOFOTENS

10   0   10   20
MILES

VAERÖY

Refreshed by this welcome break, they turned their attention to Gjeit-galjar Tind. Throughout most of their stay the jagged pinnacles of this mountain had been hidden by mist. From the seashore it looked the most difficult of the three major peaks, but in fact it turned out to be the easiest to climb. Their route led up a deep gully partly filled with snow which took them to a small snow field behind the summit. From the snow field the top was easily reached over large slabs of rock piled one on top of the other. The topmost slab provided an exposed stance from the edge of which boulders could be dropped for hundreds of feet down the east face without striking the vertical sides of the mountain. Their Norwegian porter built a cairn seven feet high to proclaim to future mountaineers that this summit had been conquered.

On August 14, they broke camp, returning to Svolvaer after a pleasant sail through the outer islands. At Svolvaer Hastings left the group, but Collie, Woolley and Priestman visited Digermulen on the Raftsund. They walked up to a small mountain lake hidden away by surrounding preci-pices, with a wild beauty that reminded Collie of Loch Coruisk in his beloved Cuillin of Skye. From Digermulen they attempted an unnamed peak in bad weather and low clouds. This involved a steep climb up to a rocky ridge joining their peak with the Troltinder, but having reached a gap in the ridge they decided not to risk the precipitous west face in such weather. They turned back in pouring rain, thus ending the season's climbing.

In the summer of 1903 Collie went back with Slingsby to the Lofoten Islands. From Svolvaer they took the local steamer to Moskenes the last and loneliest of the big islands. There they camped at the head of a fjord with vertical cliffs all round them and occasional waterfalls coming down hundreds of feet into the fjord. They had great difficulty finding a place for the tents, but finally found a small patch of nearly flat grass between great stretches of glacier-worn rock. There they stayed for about ten days with perfect weather and of course continuous daylight. The only drawback to Moskenes was the absence of bushes on the island. Wood for cooking was brought in ships for a hundred miles from the mainland. After the Canadian Rockies it was a great change for Collie to have to buy small pieces of wood almost a foot long by three inches thick, and then row them in a boat for miles to the campsite. Wood was almost as expen-sive as food, and Collie regretted that the biscuits were not more inflam-mable so that they could be used as a cheap substitute for wood.

They made a few modest climbs. The most impressive was Hermandaals Tind which they ascended by a rocky ridge with a gap in it. At the gap they found a perpendicular couloir running down the west face for nearly 3000 feet. If either of them had fallen when crossing the couloir, they would have fallen straight into the sea without touching the sides. It was a terrifying spot which they were glad to be out of. In between ascents they enjoyed sea fishing. The greatest fun was provided by octopus which squirted torrents of water over the fishermen when caught and occasionally a black inklike fluid. In addition they caught cod and other fish which were plentiful in these waters.

From Moskenes they returned to Svolvaer. Rulten, still unclimbed since Collie's previous attempt in 1901, beckoned them on. The climbing was splendid but severe; mostly bare rock set at a steep angle. The last eleven hundred feet took them eight hours of continuous climbing. At the top they found they were on the lowest of two peaks with no chance of getting from one to the other. A huge couloir filled with ice and snow separated the two. Two days later they struggled a long way up this couloir but without success. Dejected at their failure they returned to Svolvaer. Collie refused to believe that the eastern peak was impossible and returned to the attack. He described their eventual triumph in a letter to Thompson:

> There was a hopeless looking arête on the east we had not tried, so we thought we would go back and have one more try. The result was most unexpected. For on one place on this arête that from below was perpendicular, we found running right up the nose of the arête a small gully; this enabled us to get a long way on. Another very nasty dip we managed to turn by descending some distance down the southern face and then traversing, before finally reaching the top. Both peaks gave us magnificent rock work and there are no easy ways up at all.[4]

To celebrate their success, they hired a small cutter which had been fitted with a petrol engine and went for a long cruise. They nearly got wrecked, for the tides that ran between the islands were strong and the engine had a way of suddenly quitting. At such times the boat, caught in the rushing tide, was tossed about and spun round and round like a tree trunk in a whirlpool. If the boat had touched any submerged rocks it would have been ripped to pieces. Fortunately they had a first-class old fisherman on board who put up some sails and saved them from disaster. Collie regarded this exciting episode with the same enthusiasm as he had his canoeing adventure on the Neckar River in 1883.

Their last climb was up the highest peak in the Lofoten Islands, Mösadlen, about 4300 feet. It had been climbed before and was not difficult. From the summit, in absolutely clear weather, they recognized the Tränen Islands almost 190 miles away. It was a fitting climax to their holiday which had included one of Collie's most difficult climbs, the west peak of Rulten. It compared for degree of severity with many of his climbs in the Alps.

In 1904 he returned for a last visit to the Lofoten Islands with Slingsby, Woolley and Dr. J. Collier. Together they climbed Biskops Hue (the Mitre), Hermans Tind, Kjoendals Noebbe, Klokke Tind, Langstrand Tind and Olstind. The chapter which Collie devoted to these islands in his book *Climbing on the Himalaya and Other Mountains* is an eloquent expression of the appeal they made to him. For sheer climbing pleasure they undoubtedly ranked in his mind second only to Skye.

Chapter Nine
North of the Yellowhead

North of the Yellowhead

After several seasons of climbing in the Lofoten Islands, the Italian Alps, and the Cuillin of Skye, Collie returned to the Canadian Rockies in 1910, accompanied by Arnold Mumm, another distinguished Victorian mountaineer. The times were changing very rapidly in the Canadian mountaineering world. Since Collie's first visit in 1897, all the major accessible peaks had been climbed. The Dominion surveyors, following in the footsteps of the railroad surveyors, had mapped large areas. The books of climbing pioneers such as Collie, Stutfield, Wilcox, Outram and Coleman, together with an active promotion campaign by the Canadian Pacific Railway, which included providing mountain guides, building hotels, and encouraging famous mountaineers such as Whymper to visit, were attracting ever increasing numbers of tourists to this area.

The Alpine Club of Canada played a significant part in the early development of the mountains. Founded in 1906, it rapidly expanded under the vigorous leadership of A.0. Wheeler, a Dominion surveyor living in Banff. At each of its first three summer camps at Yoho Pass, Paradise Valley, and Rogers Pass about fifty initiates completed the graduating climbs. The Club built and furnished a clubhouse in Banff, complete with meeting rooms, a library, smoking room and a few bedrooms, where Canadian mountaineers could gather and on occasion entertain their guests from overseas. The Club numbered 523 members in 1909 when it held its fourth annual camp at Lake O'Hara.

A strong British contingent was led by Professor H.B. Dixon, who had accompanied Collie on his first Canadian expedition; Edward Whymper was also on hand. Although Collie had been appointed one of the London committee members for the Club in 1908, he serving as chairman and Mumm as secretary, he would not have enjoyed attending a camp of this nature. Accustomed to roughing it in small groups of dedicated mountaineers, he would have been appalled at the conglomeration of sixty tents and over two hundred people. The presence of fifty women, a sure sign of the changing times, would have only added to his disquietude. There is no record of him climbing with a woman in the party since the Alpine expeditions with Lily Bristow in 1893.

Mumm's experiences in the Rockies in 1909 were to provide the impetus for Collie's return the next year. Like Collie, Mumm had climbed in the Lake District of England, in the Alps, and in the Himalaya. With Dr. T.G. Longstaff, Major Bruce and three Swiss guides he had attempted, in 1907, the ascent of Trisul (23,406 feet), the highest peak then attained by man. Mumm reached a height of over 20,000 feet before being disabled by illness. Longstaff continued to the summit with two Alpine guides and one native porter. A man of independent means, Mumm was able to afford his own personal guide, Moritz Inderbinen. For twenty years they climbed together in a master-servant relationship almost feudal in nature and fast disappearing in the late Victorian era. He was joined for the Canadian climbing by Geoffrey Hastings and Leo Amery. Their target: Mount Robson, the highest peak in the Canadian Rockies.

The territory near Robson to the north of Lake Louise had been opened up by the construction of the Grand Trunk Railway. The survey route passed through Edmonton, and headed due west to enter the mountains at Brulé Lake. Thence it passed along the shores of Jasper Lake, through the site of present-day Jasper, and up the Miette River to the Yellowhead Pass. From there it followed the Fraser River down through Tête Jaune Cache to Kamloops. The eastern approaches of the Yellowhead were fairly wide and thinly timbered, but to the west of the Great Divide overgrowth was heavy. Lord Milton and Dr. Cheadle, the first tourists in western Canada, described some of the horrors of a journey through the Yellowhead Pass in 1863:

> The road we had come was the worst we had yet had, awful fallen timber; the two men with axes ahead of us all the time; frequently had to leap the horses over fallen timber, lots of rocky ground; up a narrow defile between high hills resembling Yorkshire, but sometimes covered with pine. Crossed the Miette and its branches six times in the course of the afternoon; the last very difficult, tremendous falls, immense rocks, something like the wharf just below the Strid . . . Whole country seems to be burnt and we shall probably have some difficulties with fallen timber for some time.[1]

The first party to explore north of the Yellowhead, in 1907, consisted of the Coleman brothers, A.P. and L.Q., who had been tramping in the Canadian Rockies since the 1880's, the Rev. G.B. Kinney, a cook, and a pack train of ten horses. Leaving from Laggan, they travelled to the Yellowhead through the valleys of the Pipestone, Siffleur, Saskatchewan, Sunwapta, Athabasca and Miette rivers. This was the first overland Banff-to-Jasper expedition and followed, for part of the way, the present highway. From the mouth of the Grand Forks of the Fraser, they had to hack their way through fallen timber to reach a camp near the base of Mount Robson. The journey took a little over one month. From their base camp they spent two days exploring the slopes of the mountain, but foul weather drove them back.

The next year the same three mountaineers, accompanied by John Yates, a well-known packer from Lac St. Anne on August 30, established a permanent camp on the east side of Mount Robson. For nineteen days, frustrated by storms and blizzards, they explored the eastern approaches to Robson, climbing three virgin peaks in the process. On one occasion they spent twelve and a half hours climbing up the Robson Glacier to an altitude of 10,500 feet, only to be forced to retreat by the lateness of the hour. Two subsequent attempts to climb the glacier were defeated by bad weather. Making one last desperate effort by himself, Kinney climbed to a height of nearly 10,000 feet over the rocks of the great north shoulder. Driven back by a fearful wind, he regained the campfire in the valley after an absence of thirty hours. Two days later the three climbers attacked Mount Robson from a different angle, up steep slopes of ice and snow to an estimated height of 11,700 feet. Again the lateness of the hour caused them to turn back. Thus ended all attempts on the mountain for 1908.

In May 1909 Kinney, then living in Victoria, received a telegram informing him that "foreign parties" had designs on Mount Robson. Frantic with fear that he might be beaten to the summit, he hastily organized an outfit on a shoestring budget. Setting out from Edmonton on June 11, he slowly made his way west on horseback over terrain made almost impassable by heavy floods. He met up with Donald ("Curly") Phillips, a sturdy youth of twenty-five who was exploring the country for future guiding prospects. Desperately short of food, and with only a crooked rifle to provide an uncertain supply of wild game, the two men pushed on up the Moose Pass, circled round the north of Robson past Adolphus Lake and Berg Lake, and on July 24 were camped below the northwest cliffs of Mount Robson. After repeated heroic efforts, interrupted by frequent storms, Kinney and Phillips on August 13 arrived within a short distance of the summit, which Kinney claimed to have captured "for my own country and for the Alpine Club of Canada."

The "foreign party" which had sent Kinney racing for Mount Robson was that of Mumm, Hastings, Amery, Inderbinen, and their guide John Yates. After briefly visiting the Canadian Alpine Club camp at Lake O'Hara, these climbers had set off along the Grand Trunk survey route to Mount Robson. At the ferry above Jasper Lake, on August 23, they met Kinney, who claimed to have reached the summit. Not until fifty years later did he admit otherwise, though doubts were raised by Phillips' remarks. In spite of their disappointment the British party (from the upper reaches of the Moose River), carried out an exhausting and unproductive twenty-nine hour reconnaissance of Mount Robson. This exploit had only been beaten once in the memory of the trio of climbers, and that was Hastings' thirty-five hours out on Nanga Parbat. A more productive exploration was from the top of the east fork, which took them up a snow trough between the Helmet, a subsidiary peak, and the massive ice slopes of the eastern wall. They turned back just in time to avoid an avalanche which would have swept them to their death. Bad weather set in and the climbing season for 1909 was at an end.

When Mumm returned to London with the news of this new mountaineering area opened up by the approach of the Grand Trunk Railroad, Collie decided to try his hand once more at a Canadian adventure. Collie, Mumm, and Inderbinen were the climbers; Fred Stephens was in charge of the outfit; Yates, who was very familiar with this northern country, Allan McConachie and George Swain made up the trail crew. They set out from Wolf Creek, near present-day Edson, on July 17, 1910. The advent of the railroad had spared them many miles of dreary travelling through the deep mud of the forest trails from Edmonton to Jasper. This trail had been so wearisome the year before that Amery had had to dangle a photograph of Mount Robson in front of Mumm, like a carrot in front of a donkey, to prevent him from turning back.

The first few days were spent ascending the MacLeod River, then crossing over a high divide into the Athabasca Valley. Two more days brought them past Folding Mountain to the foot of Roche Miette where the Athabasca flows out right under the mountain. A little farther on, on the far bank of the river was the site of Jasper House, the Hudson's Bay post established in this region by Jasper Hawse in 1800. The old House had been torn down to provide firewood for the railroad surveying parties.

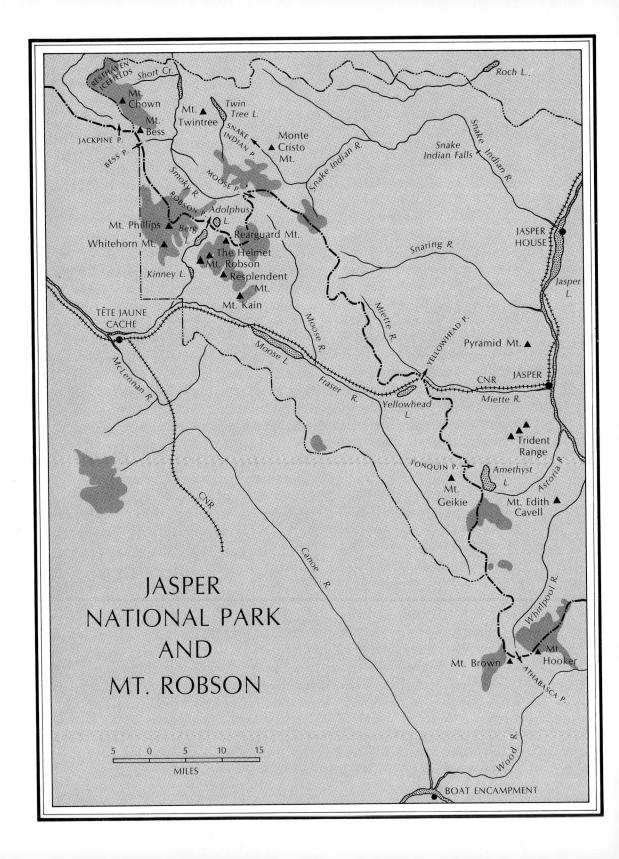

RESTHAVEN
ICEFIELDS
Short Cr.
Roch L.

▲ Mt.
Chown
Mt. ▲
Twintree
Twin
Tree L.
JACKPINE P.
Mt. ▲
Bess
Monte ▲
Cristo
Mt.

SNAKE
INDIAN P.
Snake Indian R.
BESS P.
Snake
Indian Falls
Snake Indian R.

Smoky R.
MOOSE P.
ROBSON P.
*Adolphus
L.*
JASPER
HOUSE

Mt. Phillips ▲
*Berg
L.*
Rearguard Mt.
Whitehorn Mt. ▲
The Helmet ▲
Mt. Robson
Snaring R.
Jasper
L.

Kinney L.
▲ Resplendent
Mt.
▲ Mt. Kain
Moose R.
Miette R.

TÊTE JAUNE
CACHE
YELLOWHEAD P.
Pyramid Mt. ▲

McLennan R.
Moose L.
Fraser R.
CNR
JASPER

*Yellowhead
L.*
Miette R.

CNR
▲▲
▲ Trident
Range

TONQUIN P.
*Amethyst
L.*
Canoe R.
Astoria R.

▲ Mt.
Geikie
Mt. Edith ▲
Cavell

JASPER
NATIONAL PARK
AND
MT. ROBSON

Whirlpool R.

▲ Mt.
Hooker
Mt. Brown ▲
ATHABASCA P.

*Wood
R.*

5 0 5 10 15
MILES

BOAT ENCAMPMENT

Above this site the Athabasca spread out into Jasper Lake, ten miles long by three miles wide, surrounded by the rugged red rocks of Pyramid Mountain to the west, and the clean-cut grey rocks of the Miette, Jacques, and Colin ranges to the east. Above Jasper Lake lived two or three families of half-breeds, descendants of old-time employees of the Company, who helped the party cross the river in dugout canoes.

Near the site of Henry House, the old North-West fur trading company post, and lying close to the shelter of the Palisades, they came to the cabin of a homesteader named Swift. Swift, an enterprising and optimistic American, had in fifteen years become very much of a local institution. He had cleared and irrigated the land, and in the midst of the wilderness was able to furnish exhausted and often desperately hungry travellers with eggs, milk, meat, potatoes and flour. He was a mine of information about all the happenings in the backwoods, and entertained his visitors with spicy anecdotes of his early days in the wild west.

At the present townsite of Jasper, the party turned west to follow the Miette up a pleasant valley to the Yellowhead Pass. The route was now clearly marked by the railroad surveyors, so that by August 1, they arrived at Moose Lake on the far side of the Yellowhead Pass. They had travelled one hundred and fifty miles on horseback in fifteen days. From a spot near the junction of the Moose and Fraser rivers, they had their first view of the distant snowcapped summit of Mount Robson. They then struck northward up the broad Moose Valley, following the east fork up to Moose Pass (6570 feet), about ten miles northeast of Mount Robson. This was the route used by the Colemans and Yates two years previously. From Moose Pass the trail turned due west to descend to the headwaters of the Smoky River. On August 9, they established camp near Berg Lake. The floating blocks of ice that dot its surface are carved from the mighty Berg Glacier which sweeps down 7000 feet from the summit of Robson, and gives the lake its name.

From the northwest shore of the lake, the gigantic Robson massif rises up on the far side from Rearguard to Extinguisher, the Helmet and finally the pure white summit of Robson. This northwest face of the mountain sweeping down into Berg Lake is one of the most spectacular views in the Rockies, its only close rivals being Lake Louise, Lake O'Hara and Mount Assiniboine. Among the wonders on this northwest face of Robson is the play of colours on the white ice and snow as the setting sun on a clear evening bathes the upper precipices in orange, gold and pink, while the lower slopes are in purple. At all hours, but mostly in the late afternoon and early evening, when the hot sun has done its work, the mighty cliffs ring out with the thunder of avalanches or the sharp cracks of the Berg Glacier breaking into more blocks of ice. Like many solitary peaks, Mount Robson generates its own weather system, and as often as not, the peak is hidden in cloud, mist, or driving storms.

Tackling Mount Robson, which Collie described as being 13,700 feet, but which has since been scaled down to 12,972 feet, was an ambitious project for a man fifty-one years old, but given good weather, it was well within his capabilities. Like most mountaineers at that time, Collie preferred unscaled peaks; each of his climbs in Canada was a first ascent. It may be that he did not regard Kinney's claim too seriously; certainly A.O. Wheeler, director of the Alpine Club of Canada, did not; in 1913 he picked a crack team to make sure of the peak for the Club. If Collie had had better luck with the weather in 1910, he might have added this outstanding peak to his notable collection of Canadian summits.

As it was, the weather remained too unsettled for any serious attempt on Robson, and Collie was not one to stage heroics in the face of blizzards and driving rainstorms. Instead the party turned to lesser peaks. They climbed Mumm Peak (9718 feet), lying immediately north of Berg Lake, from the south by the scree slopes rising up from Robson Pass, and thence by a short chimney to the summit; then climbed Mount Phillips (10,660 feet), situated a few miles west of Berg Lake by ascending the east glacier of the peak; and made an unsuccessful attempt on Mount Resplendent (11,240 feet), three miles southeast of Mount Robson. A heavy snowstorm on August 22 completely destroyed their hopes of climbing Robson. They then decided to head north up the Smoky River and explore some of the side valleys which might lead to the Pacific watershed. Their second attempt at following a large stream westward led them up to a splendid mountain with almost perpendicular limestone precipices and a large glacier on the east side. On the south side of this mountain, named Mount Bess by Yates, was an easy pass over the watershed into British Columbia.

It was now necessary to return to civilization. Yates had heard from some Indians that a pass connected the Smoky River with the headwaters of the Snake Indian River (then known as the Stoney River), but none of the party had travelled through it. They decided to rely on Yates' excellent judgment as a trail finder, though if they missed the Snake Indian River they would most likely finish up on the Sulphur River far to the north and hundreds of miles from Edmonton. On September 2, they started down the Smoky Valley and turned east up the first promising-looking valley.

Here they came to a beautiful lake with two small islands, each with a single fir tree growing on it. Twintree Lake, as it was naturally named, was situated ten miles north of Moose Pass, the route by which they had first entered this country. Yates refused to follow this valley to its head, but turned up a side valley to the east. Two days later they crossed an easy pass above tree line, over miles of rolling grass uplands, and descended on the other side to a stream which turned out to be the Snake Indian River. By following this river, in dismal weather with several snowstorms, they reached the Athabasca River at the foot of Brulé Lake on September 16. Their discovery of one hundred miles of relatively easy trail into new country, together with the challenge of Mount Bess, decided the issue for 1911. They would return to the country north of the Yellowhead.

On July 24, 1911, the same party with the addition of J. Smith, an expert axeman, set off from the Athabasca up the Snake Indian River. It took seven days to cut out the first twenty-five miles of trail through fallen and burnt timber. Once past this obstacle, Smith returned to civilization. One day, while resting at the side of the trail, they found an old weatherbeaten inscription on a tree trunk, which read, "Jack Grame and Archie Turnbull May 20, 1895," evidence that white men, possibly trappers, had passed this way before.

They camped at the summit of the Snake Indian Pass for three days so that Collie could climb a neighbouring peak and start his plane table survey of distant mountains. The survey work and photography which went hand in hand with all Collie's explorations in the Canadian Rockies involved considerable sacrifice in carrying the heavy equipment of those days for hundreds of miles on horseback and then up various peaks. Admittedly the sacrifice was not made entirely by Collie, for there were always sturdy helpers, but he provided the inspiration for this extra effort. The survey peak was named Mount Hoodoo in honour of Yates' courageous and determined bulldog, which had to be roped up the last 600 feet to the rocky summit. The plucky bulldog twice made the journey from Lac St. Anne to the Rockies and back on foot. It is therefore a pity that the name Mount Hoodoo has not survived; it was possibly the one now known as Monte Cristo Mountain. From the summit at 9460 feet, they had an uninterrupted view for miles in every direction. Mount Bess, discovered the year before, proved to be the southernmost peak of a group of high snow mountains with several glaciers leading down into creeks draining towards the Smoky River. A peak a little to the north of Mount Bess appeared to be the highest in this group, and it was towards this mountain that they next made their way.

On August 11, after descending to the Smoky River, they camped at the head of a creek, possibly Short Creek, which runs down from the Resthaven Ice Field. There was ample evidence that the glacier was still advancing, and that the retreat now characteristic of Canadian glaciers had not yet set in. With difficulty they found a route up the icefalls and on August 18, starting before sunrise, they climbed up to an extensive snow plateau surrounded by rock and snow peaks. Crossing the plain to the west, they led up to a snow col between two peaks, thence along an arête to the north until they reached the top of an unnamed peak 10,200 feet high.

Collie was most impressed with the view to the west and southwest, from the range of mountains between the main chain and the Fraser Valley to the faraway range of the Cariboo Mountains.

> This mountain land in the near future should prove a great field for mountain exploration. At the present time it is practically impossible to get at; even the hardy prospector has never penetrated into its fastnesses. The dense western forests with their fallen trees, thick underbrush full of devil's club, and the turbulent glacier streams have stopped even the most venturesome. It will . . . be well worth accomplishing, for the Cariboo mountains, in my opinion, are a finer range than the Selkirks, they are probably higher, and the peaks are very beautifully-shaped mountains.[2]

On August 22, they started down the valley, intending to head northward along the Smoky River and explore other creeks flowing in from the west. Confronted with deadfall, burnt timber and muskeg, they were forced to turn back and use the remaining time more profitably exploring Mount Bess, which they ascended on August 26. Not a breath of wind was stirring when they reached the summit, from which they could see mountains for 100 miles in every direction. For the first time, Collie saw to the east "the level pine woods stretching away to the prairie." Two peaks in the Cariboo range, and one far away to the south in the Selwyn range, were especially fine. The Robson massif and Mount Geikie towered up; "a shapely snow pyramid" in the dim distance was almost certainly Mount Columbia. "Out of the innumerable peaks that we could see spread out before us," Collie noted, "only two, Mount Columbia and Mount Robson, had ever been climbed by anyone except ourselves."

The Bess Pass which they followed into British Columbia turned out to be an old Indian trail, seemingly once important, for in many places it cut deeply into the moss and earth, but unused for perhaps thirty years. Teepee poles left embedded at a campsite near the summit of the pass were quite rotten. West of the pass the trail turned north, crossing a spur of Mount Bess, and then rising to cross Jackpine Valley. Above tree level to the west of Mount Bess, and lying north of Horse Creek, lay an attractive rolling meadow, resembling a Scottish moor except that it was covered with grass. Here the travellers walked with ease, admiring the great snow-clad peaks and the deep pine-clad valleys.

Reluctantly, as if sensing that this would be his last chance to admire the beauty of these mountains and to share the warmth and companionship of the campfire, Collie ordered the party to start on the trail for home. The weather continued clear, the finest in six summers of travel in the Rockies, with the valleys free of snow. It was a fitting farewell trip down the Snake Indian River. On September 15, they crossed the Athabasca River at Prairie Creek and shortly thereafter Collie, Mumm, and Inderbinen boarded the eastbound train.

The expedition had been on the trail for sixty days, had travelled at least 250 miles, and had mapped out an area of at least 400 square miles. This journey, as all of Collie's in Canada, was through a wilderness area almost untouched by man. The trails he blazed, the passes, the lakes, and the mountains he named are commemorated to this day in the Dominion Survey maps. In spite of his gloomy predictions that the Canadian Rockies would be overrun by tourists in the same way as Switzerland had been, the country north of the Yellowhead remained largely inviolate. A road open only to horses and hikers leads up to Kinney Lake and thence by a steep climbing trail to Berg Lake, where Roy Hargreaves built a primitive log chalet entirely in keeping with its surroundings, in the 1920's. The old routes by the Snake Indian River or Moose Pass are now seldom used. Occasionally tents blossom forth like summer flowers on the shores of Lake Adolphus, and like summer flowers quickly vanish. Mount Robson still presents a formidable mountaineering challenge, although now more because of vagaries of the weather than technical problems. The Ralph Forster hut, built in 1969, will at least spare future generations of climbers the rugged discomforts of bivouacs at high altitude experienced so often by the Rev. Kinney.

As he boarded the train to return to civilization, after what proved to be his last summer of exploration, Collie was saddened to think that

no longer should we sit over the campfires in our tent and listen to the stories of Fred Stephens about bear hunts, prospectors, hunters, and the endless other subjects that are of interest to the dwellers in the wilds. No longer should we laugh over the small jokes and the happenings that go to make up life in camp; we were soon to be engulfed by the great whirlpool of everyday life where the dollar counts for more than the man, and where the chains of custom bind one to the conventional life of civilized society. Those who have never tasted the freedom of camp life amongst the great mountains can hardly understand the immense peacefulness that it all means. One does not trouble much either about the yesterdays or the to-morrows, and the hours do not fall heavily. Yes, the camp life is healthy for both mind and body, and the wanderer amongst the great mountains can sleep peacefully and dream of the snows and mighty woods, of the rushing rivers, and the clear lakes reflecting the white clouds, and the rock peaks, and can feel with far more certainty than most that "all's well with the world."[3]

Chapter Ten
The Later Years

The Later Years

The Canadian expedition of 1911 marked the end of Collie's mountain explorations. Had he suspected this at the time he would have found life unbearable, but on his return to England he found himself caught up in the ever-increasing pressure of work. After having held an appointment as professor of chemistry at the College of the Pharmaceutical Society, London from 1896, he had succeeded Sir William Ramsay in 1902 as professor of organic chemistry and in 1913 as director of the chemical laboratories at University College of the University of London. By then he had published sixty-two scientific papers, on his own or in collaboration with other workers, and added sixteen after 1913. He retired from the college with the rank of Professor Emeritus in 1911, but continued to work in the laboratories until 1922, when at the age of seventy-four he gave up all scientific work.

Collie's most significant work was in the field of organic chemistry. The subjects are so technical that only brief reference will be made to them. He was the first to suggest the formula for benzene, which was familiarly known in the laboratory as the "Collywobble." His work on benzene and other naturally occurring compounds, usually in very small quantities, led him to develop the semimicro methods of analysis which have been so successfully applied in the field of medical biochemistry. Another part of his work brought him in contact with dyes. From this must have stemmed his interest in the colouring of Chinese glazes on pottery and porcelain, the topic of three scientific papers. He was appointed a Fellow of the Chemical Society in 1885, joined the Council of that Society in 1889, and became its Vice-President in 1909.

As Director of the chemical laboratories he built up a first-class school of organic chemistry which trained many men of high distinction. To them he was the "Old Man," a title of which he was very proud. Professor Smiles, one of his pupils, compared him to a landscape gardener because of the broad view he took of his subject. "He was no specialist. Anything which savoured of narrowness was repugnant to his nature, but he was a true philosopher. It was this that made his lectures and his teaching so interesting, for there always seemed to be something intriguing beyond the horizon of what he was saying."[1]

Collie was a skillful experimenter who constructed his own glass apparatus, including vacuum tubes in which gases could be exposed to electrical discharges. He collaborated with Ramsay in work on argon and helium, and made the first neon light. While working with Hubert Patterson, Collie detected the presence of neon after the passage of an electrical discharge through hydrogen at low pressure. This transmutation of a new chemical element could not at first be repeated by other investigators, and the effect was thought to be due to leakage of air into the vacuum tubes or evolution of neon from the electrodes. In later experiments Collie proved that there was no leakage of air, and by eliminating the electrodes showed that they were not a source of contamination. Because these experiments were carried out in Ramsay's laboratories, the credit for discovering neon in 1898 has gone to him instead of to Collie. Collie's claim to the discovery was attested to in a letter written by his old chief, Professor Edmund A. Letts, on the occasion of his receiving the Honorary degree of Doctor of Science from the University of Belfast on July 9, 1913. To the university authorities Professor Letts wrote that:

Professor Collie was not only my assistant here but also my pupil for some years at the University College, Bristol, and it was because of the high opinion I had formed of him in the latter capacity that I invited him to come over and help me. That he has more than fulfilled the high expectations I had of him goes, I think, without saying, and I should like to avail myself of this opportunity to state that since we decided to make him one of our alumni, he has I believe, added to his laurels by his most recent work, in collaboration with Mr. Patterson, published only a few years ago. It is of course, premature to speak with certainty of the outcome of these researches as amounting to an actual synthesis of a so-called chemical element, but at least it looks very much like it.[2]

There is no reference to Ramsay, and his credit for the discovery of neon, as Collie pointed out in a personal statement, was entirely unearned.

Another example of Collie's versatility was the occasion on which he took the first X-ray photograph for medical diagnostic purposes. The X-ray or Roentgen ray was discovered by the noted German physicist Wilhelm Conrad Roentgen in 1895, when he was engaged in research at Würzburg University. For his discovery Roentgen was awarded the first Nobel Prize in Physics in 1901. With his contacts at Würzburg University, Collie would have been kept well informed of the developments in this field. His research work with the passage of electrical discharges through glass vacuum tubes gave him the technical ability to reproduce Roentgen's work. His skill, original thinking and interest in photography were called into play when University College Hospital sent him a patient who was thought to have a fragment of a needle in her thumb. Collie placed the thumb on a photographic plate and exposed it to Roentgen's rays. The developed plate showed the exact position of the needle. With regard to his scientific work Collie once observed in a typically sardonic aside: "If anyone happens to write an obituary for me, I want two things said—I first discovered neon and I took the first X-ray photograph." For neither of these has he received full recognition.

Collie received three honorary degrees from British universities in addition to the one from Belfast. The citations and the occasions on which these were granted give some indication of the high regard in which he was held in academic circles. On Tuesday April 23, 1907, the University of Glasgow held an Honorary Graduation at the opening of the new science buildings. The recipients of Honorary degrees included the Prince and Princess of Wales (later King George V and Queen Mary), the Duke of Argyll, the Earl of Elgin and Earl Roberts of Kandahar. Collie was presented before the distinguished assembly for his LL.D degree as a scientist, author, geographer and explorer. In 1913 he was honored by the University of Liverpool, from which he received the Honorary degree of Doctor of Science. The citation, only part of which has been preserved, is couched in flowery language which must have made Collie blush. "Doctor Collie is one of the magicians who have transformed science into a bewildering romance. Under their spell the solid world dissolves; its essential constituents change and blend, and the integrity even of the precious metals is assailed." He was further described as "one of the leading lights of science in England."

The last Honorary degree was the LL.D presented by the University of St. Andrews on November 3, 1926. This ceremony was designed to honour explorers. The Honorary graduands included Dr. Fridtjof Nansen, the famous Arctic explorer; Captain Otto Neumann Sverdrup, the skipper of Nansen's ship the "Fram"; Professor Vilhelm Bjerknes, director of meteo-

CARTOON No. 10.

THE SUBSTANCE—"THE OLD MAN."

rology at the University of Bergen, who had developed new methods of weather forecasting; and Colonel Sir Tannatt W.E. David, Professor of Geology at the University of Sydney, who had sailed with Shackleton in the British Antarctic Expedition of 1907-1909. To these distinguished names were added those of General the Hon. Charles Granville Bruce and Professor John Norman Collie. What a great moment it must have been for these two men who had been friends for thirty years. Bruce was being honoured for leading the Everest Expeditions of 1922 and 1924, Collie for his achievements in mountaineering and exploration.

After his work with Conway's and Mummery's expeditions to the Himalaya in the 1890's, Bruce had continued climbing. Two members of the 1922 Everest Expedition led by Bruce had climbed to a height of 27,300 feet using oxygen. General Bruce had again been in charge of the 1924 Everest Expedition, but fell ill of malaria on the approach march through Tibet. Collie, an original member of the Mount Everest Committee, which had been founded by the Royal Geographical Society and the Alpine Club in 1920, had succeeded Sir Francis Younghusband as chairman in 1923. As chairman of the Committee, he had authorized his old friend Bruce to accept the leadership of the Everest Expedition of 1924. As he listened to the address to the graduands, given by Nansen, he must have had poignant memories of Mummery's loss some thirty years earlier.

Collie continued his summer visits to Skye for the rest of his life. For many years, he and the painter Colin Phillip rented Glen Brittle House near the southwestern end of the Cuillin. There Collie was at his best, a charming host, ready to gratify his guests' desires whether for climbing, fishing or shooting. He was a good shot and enjoyed shooting grouse on the moors, but he refused to take part in deer stalking. Each season he asked his friends to undertake the task of bagging the number of stags specified in the lease. One day, when asked why he never shot a stag, he replied, "too high up the scale, my friend." The proximity of Glen Brittle House to the Cuillin attracted many members of the climbing fraternity. If no beds were available, the guests slept on the smoking-room floor. Whenever Collie was in residence, John Mackenzie was invariably with him, and together they led visitors up challenging and fascinating climbs.

Collie wrote extensively about his climbing and exploration, contributing twenty-four articles to mountaineering and geographical journals, and publishing two books, *Climbing on the Himalaya and Other Mountain Ranges* (1902), and *Climbs and Explorations in the Canadian Rockies*, written in collaboration with Stutfield (1903). One of his most interesting experiences in the mountains was related to the annual dinner of the Cairngorm Club, of which he was the Honorary President.[3] Many years before, Collie had been climbing Ben Macdhui, the highest of the Cairngorm Mountains. He was returning from the summit cairn in a mist when he thought he heard something other than the noise of his own footsteps in the snow. For every few steps he took he heard a big crunch, and then another crunch, as if someone were walking behind him, but taking steps three or four times the length of his own. He said to himself, "This is all nonsense." He listened and heard it again, but could see nothing in the mist. As he walked on and the eerie "crunch, crunch" sounded behind him, he was seized with terror. Why, he did not know, for he did not mind being alone in the hills. But the uncanny something which he sensed sent him running, staggering blindly among the boulders, for four or five miles, nearly down to Rothie-murchas Forest. That was the last time he ever went near Ben Macdhui.

Some time later, he related his experience to Dr. A.M. Kellas, and found that he also had had a weird experience, when as a young medical student he climbed to the top of the same mountain around midnight one night in June. Dr. Kellas saw a man come up out of the Lairig Ghru and wander around the cairn near which Dr. Kellas' brother was sitting. What surprised him was that the man was practically the same height as the cairn, which was at least ten feet high, and that people did not ordinarily wander alone on the top of Ben Macdhui at midnight. The man descended into the Lairig Ghru. When Dr. Kellas asked his brother, "What on earth was that man doing walking around the cairn?", his brother replied, "I never saw any man at all." While still discussing the incident on their return journey, the brothers looked back and saw the 'giant' outlined against the skyline. As they looked he made off at a great speed until he disappeared into the valley. The authenticity of this story was confirmed in a letter written to Collie by Mr. W.G. Craigen, a lawyer in Aberdeen, and an intimate friend of Dr. Kellas.

Later still Colin Phillip met an old man, living on the edge of the Rothie-murchas Forest, who knew the Cairngorms very well. When Phillip told him the two stories, the old man was not in the least surprised, but simply replied, "Oh, aye, that would have been the Ferla Mhor [the Big Grey Man] they would have been seeing."

The publication of Collie's story in the local newspaper was followed by its widespread coverage throughout the British Isles. This in turn led to a flood of interviews and correspondence which continued for many weeks. Some of the correspondents were sceptical, but most provided corroborative evidence. Thus Professor W. Rae Sherriffs of the Department of Zoology at the University College of Southampton wrote to say that one day in July 1920 he climbed to the top of Ben Macdhui.

> I was just beginning the somewhat steep descent of the path where there is a precipitous slope to the right, and on the left far below Loch Etchachan, when I was suddenly and acutely conscious that I was not alone; that I was being followed. Something—some person or whatever it was was not far off, and it was something distinctly evil! I stopped and looked all around, but could see nothing. Everything was silent. I then continued on my way watching very carefully for the appearance of anything but saw nothing.

On his return to his lodgings in the village of Inverey, Professor Sherriffs' host informed him that the Old Grey Man of Macdhui had been seen or felt by many visitors to the mountain. The local inhabitants would not go near Macdhui. The controversy engendered by Collie's talk to the Cairngorm Club, started a legend which has persisted in Scottish climbing circles to this day.

Collie held membership in other mountaineering clubs besides the Alpine Club and the Alpine Club of Canada. He was elected a member of the Scottish Mountaineering Club in 1891, served on the Committee from 1898 to 1900 and was elected an Honorary member in 1938. In 1922 he was elected Honorary President of the Cairngorm Club, succeeding Viscount Bryce. He was very much interested in the affairs of the Club, although he seldom took part in the climbing activities. He was invited to attend a proposed excursion of the Club in June 1937 to the Shelter Stone, the scene of the founding of the Club fifty years before. The Club even offered him the use of a pony, but Collie declined, saying that he was too old for that sort of thing, and that he would have to be sure of having good weather. In 1919, however, at the age of eighty, he travelled from London to Aberdeen on the occasion of the Jubilee Dinner of the Club, and delivered an address entitled "Independence." He concluded the speech with these words:

> . . . there is an enchantment hidden away amongst the lonely expanses of the wilds. Perhaps we have inherited a belief in it from our Gaelic ancestors. It is an enchantment that can give us new knowledge, that in old age, "life's leaden metal into gold transmutes." In our youthful days we were easily made captive by these magic spells, and can lay up for ourselves fairy treasures. They are treasures that are our own; we can safely keep what we have bought; we are independent as far as they are concerned.

Collie was an Honorary member of many other climbing clubs including the American Alpine Club, the Appalachian Club and the Himalayan Club. Dr. J. Monroe Thorington of the American Alpine Club corresponded with Collie during the 1920's inviting him to return to North America, but Collie felt unable to afford the expense of a transatlantic voyage. He was elected a Fellow of the Royal Geographical Society in 1897, served twice on the Council and as Vice-President from 1924 to 1928. After being elected to the Alpine Club in 1893, he served on the Committee, became Vice-President from 1910 to 1912, and President from 1920 to 1922. Mrs. Ivor Richards (Dorothy Pilley) recalls seeing him about 1922, when he was President of the Alpine Club.

We used to see him annually at the Alpine Club tea parties in Saville Row to which ladies were invited. He was surrounded for us with the halo of the early Giants of Mountaineering. His appearance was very distinguished: spare, rugged and hawk-like, reminding one of the Sherlock Holmes drawings in the *Strand Magazine*. He was kindly to young people when we exchanged a few words which we wish we could remember.

Because of his connection with the Royal Geographical Society and the Alpine Club, Collie became an original member of the Mount Everest Committee. He tried hard to be included in the first Everest Expedition, claiming his previous Himalayan experience as justification. He was then sixty-two, and had done no serious climbing for ten years. It was just as well that he was not accepted. Of the four original climbers in the party, one never started, one died soon after entering Tibet, and one had to be invalided back to India long before he reached Everest. Collie might have been another casualty, and it probably took all of Younghusband's tact to get him to withdraw his name. As it was, the 1921 expedition nearly succeeded because of the remarkable persistence of George Leigh-Mallory, a schoolmaster at Charterhouse, and one of the finest climbers then living. After 1921 Collie never again tried to join a mountaineering expedition.

Largely through the influence of his mother, Collie had a strong sense of family kinship, which he carefully preserved throughout his life. In 1912, he handed over to Melbourne University, twenty-eight letters written by his granduncle Dr. Alexander Collie, the naval surgeon, to his grandfather George Collie of Aberdeenshire. These letters described the early founding of Western Australia. In 1936, Norman Collie completed the preservation of his granduncle's papers by depositing more letters and a

A quiet Sunday indoors at Glenbrittle Lodge, Skye. L. to R., Collie, Hastings and Slingsby

letter, Collie thanked Professor Wilsmore for a copy of the *Western Mail* containing an account of the centenary celebrations at the town of Collie in November 1935.

> I see that one person (a Mr. Wilson) suggested that the remains of Dr. Alexander Collie should be dug up and reinterred at Collie. The poor man I am sure would not like it, for he expressly asked to be buried in the same grave as a great friend of his, a native chief named Morkew. They will have to take Morkew as well to the new grave. My grandfather, Dr. A. Collie's brother, built himself a fine house on an estate in the country near Aberdeen and named the place Morkew. Some years ago, I met a man from Aberdeen, and he could not make out the name Morkew. He said it was some Gaelic word—"Mhor" for great, and "kew" was not in the Gaelic at all. I was much amused, and finally put him wise as the Americans say, but I don't think he believed me.[4]

Of Collie's immediate family, only his sister Susan Margaret, one of the first women graduates of the University of London, remained in England. After teaching for some years at Cheltenham, she moved to Bedford, where she ultimately became headmistress. Then for twenty years she was one of that distinguished band of British women—"A great headmistress of a great school." A younger brother, Alexander W. Collie, also became a schoolmaster, teaching for many years in Kashmir, and dying quite young in India. The disruptive personality in the family was Arthur Leslie Collie, nicknamed "Di". Norman Collie's letters to his mother are full of references to this unruly, selfish and extravagant young man. His excesses were all the more distressing to his brother Norman who had always worked hard, and lived on a mere pittance as a student. Di made a pretence of studying law, but although he eventually passed his exams, he never practised. Early in life, he acquired a great taste for objects of art, usually backed by sound judgment. Once in a salesroom in Bristol, he saw a picture of Martha, Mary and Christ which he believed to be a Vermeer, and bought it for ten pounds. This painting later sold for ten thousand pounds in London. With the capital, Di started his own business as an antique dealer, an occupation quite undreamed of for a gentleman in those days. His affairs prospered to such an extent that he was later employed by Cecil Rhodes to decorate and furnish the interior of Rhodes' elegant new home, Groote Shuur, near Capetown. Later on he fell out of favour with Rhodes, returned to England, and died in early middle age.

The oldest member of the family was George Henry Collie. He and Norman had the closest bonds of friendship as well as kinship, dating from the days they played together as young boys at Glassel. A shy diffident young man, Henry had been earmarked for a military career. The family's financial misfortune brought about his withdrawal from Sandhurst, and after a few years with his grandparents in Aberdeen, he left the country to seek a living in Australia. After trying his hand unsuccessfully at selling farm machinery, he moved to New Zealand. There he joined the armed Constabulary, and took part in the bloodless victory of Parihaka. The war over, he found work on a homestead, where his first job was plucking and sacking wool from dead sheep. As the wool could not come out until the sheep was in an advanced state of putrefaction, Henry was required to live by himself in a tent five miles from the homestead, and had to wash in the sea before appearing at the house to collect stores and have an occasional meal. He never quite got over his shock when the jam was put on the table in the chamber pots in which it had been preserved. His look of surprise prompted the farmer's wife to comment, "They've never been used, you know!"

Later, Henry bought a section of uncleared land near Woodville in Hawkes Bay, and over the years, he cleared the bush and established his own farm. He married the daughter of Major General Sladen, and took her to live in a small bungalow with a corrugated iron roof. The hard beginnings agreed with both of them. Henry lived to the age of eighty-seven, and his wife to ninety-five. Throughout his life, Henry looked back on the years at Glassel as the happiest in his life and named his last home "Glassel". When out riding with his young daughters, he told them of the fun he and Uncle Norman had as boys on the hills of Deeside.

In 1935 Norman accepted Henry's invitation to visit New Zealand. By the age of seventy-six, Norman had become somewhat eccentric. He is alleged to have started on the voyage with only two shirts, and of course he was attired in the famous thick tweed jacket and knickerbockers that he always wore. Three years later, he turned up at the funeral of a niece dressed in a black morning coat, orange-brown Highland tweed trousers and a very grubby macintosh. He enlivened the service by saying, "Humbug" in a perfectly audible whisper. But for all his eccentricities, he was a great favourite with his nieces and their children, by then mostly in their teens. He tipped all the children, and when one of his nieces thanked him, he replied, "I don't like doing it—but it's expected of me."

On his trip to New Zealand, he travelled down the North Island, passing through the Thermal Regions. He refused to look at the geysers and mud pools—"I am not interested in the earth's boils and sores"—he said. But at Mount Ruapehu it was a different matter. He sat for hours in the hotel window watching the lights on the mountains and the slopes below him. He loved colours as he had in his youth. When staying with his niece, Mrs. Nora Holmes, he often called the family out in the evenings to see the sunset or the lovely evening light on the cabbage trees or the lagoon. Later in the summer he visited the mountains of the South Island with his brother Henry. A picture has been preserved of them sitting comfortably relaxed outside a corrugated iron bungalow watching a pet kea (a native parrot) on the ground. The two men were remarkably alike. Long of limb, lean in build, they both had an appearance of strength and vigour that completely belied their arrival at the biblical three score years and ten. Together they relived the past as they gazed fascinated on the splendours of the Southern Alps. Norman, although he had never been in the country before, knew the names of all the main mountain peaks. How he must have longed to scale the heights. It was a magnificent setting for a farewell visit with his brother.

Collie suffered the fate of most octagenarians. He outlived nearly all his friends. Hermann Woolley, who had not commenced climbing until his fortieth year, died in 1920 at the age of seventy-four. Hugh Stutfield who had joined Collie and Woolley in all the excitement of the 1898 and 1902 expeditions to the Rockies, died in 1929. In a letter to Thompson, written as far back as 1906, Collie had complained that Woolley was getting old and that Stutfield had retired from climbing to look after his family. This process of ageing of his friends, while he remained vigorous in mind and body, was one of the causes of Collie's apparent loneliness in later years.

A last letter from Fred Stephens, Collie's guide in the Rockies, was dated July 24, 1927.[5] He wrote, "I know Doctor you are too old for any of that strenuous mountain climbing; isn't it Hell to get old when one don't want it." He described his attempts at raising foxes and how a crooked partner's running off with $1500 and the death of many foxes had left him $5000 out of pocket. He protested against the rottenness of the government, the wickedness of the Ku Klux Klan, the lying deceitful kyotes, and all the miserable grafters, game wardens and fences which interferred with a man's freedom. "Now Doctor, you know when things are going the wrong way with a fellow he isn't in the right frame of mind to write a good letter, but any way I hope to change things around and then look out for the good news. Any way we can ponder over the good times we have had, and I hope you stay well and write at least twice a year, and you and Washburn* are two of my most prized friends." This pathetic letter is a reminder of the enduring friendships which Collie made, for sixteen years after their last meeting, Fred Stephens could still pour out his troubles to this man in a distant land.

The saddest blow of all was the death of John Mackenzie of Skye in 1933. St. John Ervine had written of their friendship: "It was a pleasant and

Collie outside Sligachan Hotel in Skye in 1942 two months before his death

stimulating sight to see Collie and his friend and gillie, John Mackenzie, pacing up and down in front of Sligachan, two old men, one a distinguished scholar, the other a simple peasant, smoking their pipes and seldom speaking because their intimacy was such that it needed no words for its expression. These two men did not presume on each other. But they had a friendship that not even death, in my belief could destroy." Many friends recollect that Collie was never quite the same again after Macken-

*Stanley Washburn was a traveller, war correspondent and the author of *Trails, Trappers and Tenderfeet* (1911).

zie's death. Collie wrote the obituary for his friend, printed in the *Scottish Mountaineering Club Journal*. "There is no one who can take his place," it ended. "Those who knew him will remember him as a perfect gentleman, one who never offended by word or deed. He has left a gap that can not be filled. There was only one John, simple-minded, most lovable, and without guile. May he rest quietly in the little graveyard at Struan."

Even after the death of his close friend, Collie returned each summer to Sligachan, for Skye was home to him and his love for it was deep and everlasting. His favourite chair in the outer vestibule was known as "Collie's chair" and woe betide anyone who presumed to occupy it. From there he could look out on Glamaig and the Red Hills and down Loch Sligachan to Raasay, and envelop himself in a cloud of tobacco smoke and memories. He was intolerant of strangers, and as a result was thought rude and unfriendly. One drenching morning he was sitting in the vestibule with a friend, when two ladies approached clad in oilskins and sou'westers and armed with umbrellas. To their inquiry, "Oh, Doctor, what kind of a day will it be?" he gave no answer, but gazed out through the streaming windows. At a second venture he withdrew his pipe and without moving his gaze, replied, "Can't you use your eyes?" The ladies hastily departed.

On another occasion he was seated in the vestibule with E.C.C. Baly. On a table near them was an album of photographs of peaks in Skye. A stranger, who appeared to be a nonclimber, entered and began looking through the album. The stranger asked Collie if he had done any climbing and Collie acknowledged that he had. Pointing to a picture of a peak the man asked, "Have you climbed this one?" Collie had. Peak by peak, so to say, the man dragged out of Collie the fact that he had climbed them all. Baly could see the innocent fellow's eyes dilating with doubt. At last he pointed to an impossible-looking peak, and said, "Have you been up that?" Collie had. The man could stand it no longer. "What are you," he demanded, "a steeple jack?" Collie, who throughout had continued smoking his pipe, showed no resentment at the stranger's disbelief, nor did he attempt to prove his assertions. That was his way of doing things.

Besides John Mackenzie, Collie had two other close friends in Skye. McDonald of Tomore and John Campbell. In 1895 Sligachan Inn was owned by a syndicate which appointed John Campbell the resident manager. Some years later Campbell bought a hotel in Portree and McDonald, a member of the syndicate, undertook its management. After McDonald's death, Campbell sold the Portree Hotel and purchased Sligachan Inn, where he lived for the rest of his days. The friendship between John Campbell and Collie extended therefore over a period of almost fifty years. Campbell was the perfect example of what a host should be, and

Sligachan was a warm and friendly place under his genial direction. When Collie was beset by strangers or bored with uninteresting company, he sought refuge in Campbell's private room, called the Presbytery, where more congenial company was to be found. At the outbreak of war in 1939, Collie closed up his house in Gower Street and retired to Sligachan. Because of this he was spared the horrors of the air raids on London and the damage to his home, but not the death, early in 1940, of John Campbell. This severed the last link with the friends of his early mountaineering days.

Almost the last glimpse we have of Norman Collie is that recorded by Richard Hillary, a young fighter pilot in the Royal Air Force. In March 1941, Hillary and a friend from his squadron drove to Skye and spent a few days at Sligachan. In his book *The Last Enemy*, Hillary described meeting Collie the first night at the Inn: "we were alone in the inn save for one old man who had returned there to die. His hair was white but his face and bearing were still those of a mountaineer, though he must have been a great age. He never spoke, but appeared regularly at meals to take his place at table tight-pressed against the window, alone with his wine and his memories. We thought him rather fine." The next day the two pilots went out and climbed Bruach-na-Free. It was not a difficult climb, but developed into a fierce scramble to reach the top between two highly competitive individuals. On the way down they slipped into a pool of water and became thoroughly drenched and chilled. "Over dinner we told our landlord of our novel descent. His sole comment was 'Humph', but the old man at the window turned and smiled at us. I think he approved."

A similar misadventure had much more serious results for Collie. In the autumn of 1941, while fishing in the Storr Loch, he fell in and got a thorough wetting. The cold he took left him in poor health. Because of the stringent restrictions on travel in Skye imposed by the military authorities, he remained alone at the hotel except for occasional visits from some friends from Drynoch. His strength finally failed in the autumn of 1942. With him at the end was a friend of long standing, G.H. Lee. During his last few days his thoughts were again with his faithful friend John Mackenzie. On November 1, 1942, at the age of eighty-three, he died peacefully. At his own request, his body was laid to rest alongside John Mackenzie's grave in the little churchyard at Struan on the shore of Loch Harport. There they lie in the shadows of the mountains they loved so well.

FIRST ASCENTS IN THE CANADIAN ROCKIES
BY J. NORMAN COLLIE

1897	Mt. Lefroy	11,230 ft.	with H. B. Dixon, C. E. Fay, A. Michael, C. L. Noyes, H. C. Parker, C. S. Thompson, J. R. Vanderlip, and P. Sarbach.
	Mt. Victoria	11,365 ft.	with C. E. Fay, A. Michael, and P. Sarbach.
	Mt. Gordon	10,550 ft.	with G. P. Baker, H. B. Dixon, C. E. Fay, A. Michael, C. L. Noyes, H. C. Parker, C. S. Thompson and P. Sarbach.
	Mt. Sarbach	10,350 ft.	with G. P. Baker and P. Sarbach.
	Unnamed Peak N.E. of Mt. Thompson	9700 ft.	with G. P. Baker and P. Sarbach.
1898	Mt. Athabasca	11,452 ft.	with H. Wooley.
	Diadem Peak	11,060 ft.	with H. E. M. Stutfield and H. Woolley.
	The Snow Dome	11,340 ft.	with H. E. M. Stutfield and H. Woolley.
	Mt. Thompson	10,050 ft.	with H. E. M. Stutfield and H. Woolley.
1900	Mt. Edith	8380 ft.	with F. Stephens
1902	Mt. Murchison	10,936 ft.	with H. E. M. Stutfield, G. M. Weed, and H. Kaufmann.
	Mt. Freshfield	10,945 ft.	with J. Outram, H. E. M. Stutfield, G. M. Weed, H. Woolley, C. Kaufmann and H. Kaufmann.
	Mt. Forbes	11,852 ft.	with J. Outram, H. E. M. Stutfield, G. M. Weed, H. Woolley, C. Kaufmann and H. Kaufmann.
	Howse Peak	10,793 ft.	with H. E. M. Stutfield, G. M. Weed, H. Woolley and H. Kaufmann.

	Mt. Noyes	10,120 ft.	with H. E. M. Stutfield, G. M. Weed, and H. Woolley.
	Neptuak Peak	10,617 ft.	with H. E. M. Stutfield, G. M. Weed, H. Woolley and H. Kaufmann.
1910	Mumm Peak	9718 ft.	with A. L. Mumm and M. Inderbinen.
	Mt. Phillips	10,660 ft.	with A. L. Mumm, F. Stephens, G. Swain, J. Yates and M. Inderbinen.
1911	Hoodoo Peak (Mt. Monte Cristo)	9000 ft.	with A. L. Mumm, J. Yates and M. Inderbinen.
	Mt. Bess	10,550 ft.	with A. L. Mumm, J. Yates and M. Inderbinen.
	Unnamed	10,200 ft.	with A. L. Mumm and M. Inderbinen.

DR. J. NORMAN COLLIE.
CHRONOLOGY.

1859 Born September 10. Second son of Mr. John Collie. Mother Selina Mary, daughter of Henry Winkworth.

1861 Uncle Stephen Winkworth elected to the Alpine Club.

1865 Father retired to Glassel on Deeside.

1867 Climbed the Hill of Fare, and obtained his first view of Lochnagar.

1870 Family moved to Bristol. Sent to school at Windlesham in Surrey.

1873 Sent to Charterhouse school.

1875 Family fortunes declined. Removed from Charterhouse and sent to Clifton College.

1877 Went to University College, Bristol to study chemistry.

1878 Awarded a scholarship in chemistry. Studied under Professor Letts.

1880 Became assistant to Professor Letts at Queen's College, Belfast.

1884 Awarded the Ph.D. under Dr. Wislicenus at Würzburg University.

1885 Became Science Lecturer at Cheltenham Ladies College. Appointed Fellow of the Chemical Society.

1886 First watched Stocker and Parker climbing in Skye. Began climbing with his brother.

1888 Appointed demonstrator in chemical laboratories at University College, London. By September had ascended all the main peaks of the Cuillin in Skye, usually led by John Mackenzie.

1889 Appointed to the Council of the Chemical Society. Made the first ascent of the Basteir Tooth.

1890 Began a systematic exploration of the Cuillin Ridge with John Mackenzie.

1891 First ascent of the Thearlaich-Dubh Gap. Joined Scottish Mountaineering Club.

1892 Climbing at Chamonix. Ascent of the Brenva Mont Blanc. Traverse of the Aiguille des Charmoz with Mummery, Carr, Petherick, Pasteur, Miss Pasteur and Miss Bristow. First traverse of the Aiguille de Grépon with Hastings, Pasteur and Mummery.

1893 Elected to the Alpine Club. Ascent of the Grépon. First ascent of the Dent du Requin with Mummery, Slingsby and Hastings. First ascent of the west face of the Aiguille du Plan with Mummery, Slingsby and Hastings. Ascent of the Petit Dru. Ascent of the Matterhorn by the Italian Ridge.

1894 Climbing in Glencoe in March. First ascent from the north of the Col des Courtes. First guideless ascent of Mont Blanc by the Brenva Glacier with Mummery and Hastings. Ascent of the Aiguille Verte by the Moine Ridge. Ascent of the Matterhorn by the Zmutt Arête with Abruzzi, Mummery and Pollinger.

1895 Himalayan expedition to Nanga Parbat resulting in the death of Mummery.

1896 Elected F.R.S. Appointed Professor of Chemistry at The Pharmaceutical Society. First ascent of Sgurr Coir'an Lochain with Howell, Naismith and Mackenzie.

1897 First Canadian expedition. Appointed a Fellow of the Royal Geographical Society.

1898 Second Canadian expedition. Discovered the Columbia Ice Fields.

1899 Discovered the famous Cioch on Sron na Ciche. Spent the summer climbing in the Alps.

1900 Third Canadian expedition to the Bush River.

1901 First Lofoten expedition.

1902 Fourth Canadian expedition. Appointed Professor of Chemistry at University College. Published *Climbing on the Himalaya ... "* Appointed member of Council of Royal Geographical Society.

1903 Second Lofoten expedition. Published *Climbs and Exploration in the Canadian Rockies.*

1904 Third Lofoten expedition. Climbed in Skye with E.C. Daly and Mackenzie.

1905 Appointed to Council of Royal Society. Climbed with Woolley in the Italian Alps.

1906 Appointed Honorary member of the Canadian Alpine Club. Rented Glen Brittle House and climbed A'Chioch and the Western Gully on Sron na Ciche. Also climbed in Glencoe.

1907 Awarded the LL.D. by Glasgow University. Climbed the Amphitheatre Arête on Sron na Ciche. Rented Glen Brittle House.

1908 Officer of the local committee in London of the Canadian Alpine Club. Rented Glen Brittle House.

1909 Vice President of the Chemical Society. Rented Glen Brittle House.

1910 Fifth Canadian expedition. Elected Vice President of the Alpine Club.

1911 Sixth Canadian expedition.

1912 Read paper on "Exploration in the Rocky Mountains North of the Yellowhead Pass" to the Royal Geographical Society. Rented Glen Brittle House.

1913 Succeeded Sir William Ramsay as Director of the Chemical Laboratories at University College. Awarded Honorary degrees of D.Sc. at Queen's University, Belfast and University of Liverpool.

1914 Rented Glen Brittle House.

1915   Rented Glen Brittle House.

1920   Elected President of the Alpine Club. Herman Woolley died.

1921   Member of Council of Royal Geographical Society. Tried to join the Mount Everest expedition.

1922   Elected Honorary President of the Cairngorm Club to succeed Viscount Bryce.

1923   Succeeded Younghusband as Chairman of Mount Everest Committee.

1924   Elected Vice President of the Royal Geographical Society.

1926   Received the Honorary LL.D. at St. Andrew's University.

1927   Portrait painted in oils by A.T. Nowell.

1928   Retired from University College.

1929   Cecil Slingsby and Hugh Stutfield died.

1933   Gave up all scientific work. John Mackenzie died.

1935   Visit to New Zealand.

1938   Attended the Jubilee dinner of the Cairngorm Club at Aberdeen.

1939   Left London to live permanently in Skye.

1941   John Campbell of Sligachan died.

1942   J. Norman Collie died November 1, at Sligachan, Skye.

FOOTNOTES

Chapter 2: The British Isles

1. J.N. Collie, *Climbing on the Himalaya and other Mountain Ranges* (Edinburgh: David Douglas, 1902), p. 218.
2. Collie used Coolin and Chuilionn interchangeably. The modern spelling is Cuillin.
3. Collie, *op. cit.*, p. 222.
4. The description of John Mackenzie is derived from B.H. Humble's personal communication and his two excellent books, *The Cuillin of Skye* (London: Robert Hale Ltd., 1952), pp. 47-61 and *Tramping in Skye* (Glasgow: William MacLellan, 1947), pp. 19-20.
5. *Ibid.*.
6. J.N. Collie, "A'Chuillion," *Scottish Mountaineering Club Journal,* 4 (May, 1897), pp. 259-266.
7. Collie, *op. cit.*, p. 246.
8. *Ibid.,* pp. 257-259.
9. *Ibid.,* p. 231.
10. *Ibid.,* p. 241.
11. Collier, "The Island of Skye," *Alpine Journal,* 32 (1920), pp. 163-165.

Chapter 3: The Alps

1. A.F. Mummery, *My Climbs in the Alps and Caucasus,* 2nd ed. (London: Thomas Nelson and Sons, 1908), p. 347.
2. F.S. Smythe, *British Mountaineers* (London: Collins, 1946), p. 28.
3. Mummery, *op. cit.*, p. 36.
4. *Ibid.,* p. 171.
5. *Ibid.,* p. 215.
6. *Ibid.,* p. 223.
7. *Ibid.,* pp. 226-227.
8. J.N. Collie, *Climbing on the Himalaya and other Mountain Ranges* (Edinburgh: David Douglas, 1902), p. 176.

Chapter 4: Nanga Parbat I

1. J.N. Collie, *Climbing on the Himalaya and other Mountain Ranges* (Edinburgh: David Douglas, 1902), p. 178.
2. A.F. Mummery, *My Climbs in the Alps and Caucasus,* 2nd ed. (London: Thomas Nelson and Sons, 1908), p. 24.
3. Collie, *op. cit.*, p. 45.
4. Mummery, *op. cit.*, pp. 25-26.

Chapter 5: Nanga Parbat II

1. J.N. Collie, *Climbing on the Himalaya and other Mountain Ranges* (Edinburgh: David Douglas, 1902), p.66.

2. A.F. Mummery, *My Climbs in the Alps and Caucasus*, 2nd ed. (London: Thomas Nelson and Sons, 1908), pp. 26-27.

3. Mummery to Mr. Bryce, *The Times*, London, March, 1896.

4. Collie, *op. cit.*, p.79.

5. Mummery, *op. cit.*, p. 28.

6. Collie, *op. cit.*, p.95.

7. Mummery, *op. cit.*, pp. 33-34.

8. Collie, *op. cit.*, p. 120.

9. *Ibid.*, p.133.

Chapter 6: The Canadian Rockies, 1897-1898

1. Narrative of David Douglas, May 1, 1827, from his field journal, in the library of the Royal Horticultural Society, London. Quoted by J.M. Thorington in *A Climber's Guide to the Rocky Mountains of Canada*, 6th ed. (The American Alpine Club, 1966), p. 282.

2. H.E.M. Stutfield and J.N. Collie, *Climbs and Exploration in the Canadian Rockies* (London: Longmans, Green and Co., 1903), p.54.

3. *Appalachia*, VIII (1898), p. 9.

4. Stutfield and Collie, *op. cit.*, p. 17.

5. *Ibid.*, p. 23.

6. W.D. Wilcox, *The Rockies of Canada* (New York and London: G.P. Putnam's Sons, 1900), p. 119.

7. Stutfield and Collie, *op. cit.*, p. 30.

8. *Ibid.*, pp. 31-33.

9. J.N. Collie to C.S. Thompson, October 21, 1897. Thorington Archives, Princeton University Library. Copy in the Archives of the Canadian Rockies, Banff.

10. The Wilson Collection, Glenbow Archives, Calgary.

11. Collie to Thompson, March 23, 1898. Thorington Archives, Princeton University Library. Copy in the Archives of the Canadian Rockies, Banff.

12. *Ibid.*, May 4, 1898. Thorington Archives, Princeton University Library. Copy in the Archives of the Canadian Rockies, Banff.

13. Stutfield and Collie, *op. cit.*, p. 84.

14. *Ibid.*, p. 98.

15. J. Munro Thorington, personal communication.

16. Stutfield and Collie, *op. cit.*, p. 128.

17. *Ibid.*, pp. 128-130.

18. *Ibid.*, p. 134.

Chapter 7: The Canadian Rockies, 1900-1902

1. Jim Simpson, personal communication.

2. J.N. Collie, *Daily Journal*. Only a few pages of this journal have been found and are now in the Archives of the Canadian Rockies, Banff.

3. J.N. Collie to C.S. Thompson. Thorington Archives, Princeton University Library. Copy in the Archives of the Canadian Rockies, Banff.
4. *Ibid.*
5. H.E.M. Stutfield and J.N. Collie, *Climbs and Exploration in the Canadian Rockies* (London: Longmans, Green and Co., 1903), p. 239.
6. *Ibid.*, p. 267.
7. *Ibid.*, p. 269.
8. *Ibid.*, pp. 278-280.
9. *Ibid.*, p. 318.

Chapter 8: The Lofoten Islands

1. J.N. Collie, *Climbing on the Himalaya and other Mountain Ranges* (Edinburgh: David Douglas, 1902), p. 189.
2. *Ibid.*, p. 198.
3. *Ibid.*, p. 201.
4. Collie to Thompson, November 2, 1903. Thorington Archives, Princeton University Library. Copy in the Archives of the Canadian Rockies, Banff.

Chapter 9: North of the Yellowhead

1. W.B. Cheadle, *Cheadle's Journal of Trip Across Canada 1862-1863* (Edmonton: M.G. Hurtig Ltd., 1971, reprint), p. 170.
2. J.N. Collie, "Exploration in the Rocky Mountains North of the Yellowhead Pass," *Geographic Journal*, 39 (1912), p. 230.
3. *Ibid.*, p. 233.

Chapter 10: The Later Years

1. S. Smiles, quoted in Obituary Notices of Fellows of the Royal Society, November, 1943, p. 334.
2. Copy of Dr. Lett's letter provided by the Registrar, University of Belfast, Northern Ireland.
3. *Cairngorm Club Journal*, (July, 1926), pp. unknown.
4. *The West Australian*, March 7, 1936.
5. F. Stephens to J.N. Collie, Archives of the Canadian Rockies, Banff.

BIBLIOGRAPHY

Amery, L.S.	*Days of Fresh Air.* London: Jarrolds, 1939.
Blackshaw, A.	*Mountaineering–From Hill Walking to Alpine Climbing.* London: Penguin Books Ltd., 1970.
Clark, R.W.	*A Pictorial History of Mountaineering.* London: Hamish B. T. Batsford Ltd., 1953.
Ibid.	*Six Great Mountaineers.* London: Hamish Hamilton, 1956.
Coleman, A.P.	*The Canadian Rockies: New and Old Trails.* Toronto: Henry Froude, 1911.
Collie, J.N.	*Climbing on the Himalaya and other Mountain Ranges.* Edinburgh: David Douglas, 1902.
Cooper, D.	*Skye.* London: Routledge and Kegan Paul, 1970.
Fraser, E.	*The Canadian Rockies: Early Travels and Exploration.* Edmonton: M.G. Hurtig, 1969.
Hankinson, A.	*The First Tigers.* London: J.M. Dent and Sons Ltd., 1972.
Herrligkoffer, K.M.	*Nanga Parbat.* London: Elek Books, 1954.
Hillary, R.	*The Last Enemy.* London, Melbourne and Toronto: Macmillan, 1968.
Humble, B.H.	*The Cuillin of Skye.* London: Robert Hale Ltd., 1952.
Ibid.	*Tramping in Skye.* Glasgow: William Maclellan, 1947.
Ibid.	*The Songs of Skye.* Stirling: Eneas Mackay, 1955.
Mummery, A.F.	*My Climbs in the Alps and Caucasus,* 2nd ed. London: Thomas Nelson and Sons, 1908.
Outram, J.	*In the Heart of the Canadian Rockies.* New York and London: Macmillan, 1905.
Patton, B. and Robinson, B.	*The Canadian Rockies Trail Guide: a Hiker's Manual.* Banff: A Summerthought Publication, 1971.
Shaw, C.A.	*Tales of a Pioneer Surveyor,* Raymond Hull, ed. Toronto: Longman Canada Ltd., 1970.
Smythe, F.S.	*British Mountaineers.* London: Collins, 1946.
Stutfield, H.E.M. and Collie, J.N.	*Climbs and Exploration in the Canadian Rockies.* London: Longmans, Green and Co., 1903.
Thorington, J.M.	*The Glittering Mountains of Canada.* Philadelphia: Lea, 1925.
Ibid.	*A Climber's Guide to the Rocky Mountains of Canada,* 6th ed. U.S.A.: The American Alpine Club, 1966.

Unsworth, W.	*Tiger in the Snow: the Life and Adventures of A.F. Mummery.* London: Gollancz, 1967.
Ibid.	*Because It's There: Famous Mountaineers 1840-1940.* London: Gollancz, 1968.
Wilcox, W.D.	*The Rockies of Canada* . New York and London: G.P. Putnam's Sons, 1900.

COLLIE'S MOUNTAINEERING BIBLIOGRAPHY

"Ascent of the Dent du Requin." *Alpine Journal,* 17 (1893), pp. 9-20.

"On the Height of the Black Cuchullins in Skye." *Scottish Mountaineering Club Journal,* 2 (1893), pp. 168-173.

"Climbing near Wasdale Head." *Scottish Mountaineering Club Journal,* 3 (1894), pp. 1-9.

"On the Divine Mysteries of the Oromaniacal Quest by Orlamon Linicus." *Ibid.,* pp. 151-157.

"Climbing on the Nanga Parbat Range, Kashmir." *Alpine Journal,* 18 (1897), pp. 17-32.

"Note on a Portable Barometer." *Geographical Journal,* 10 (1897), p. 206.

"A'Chullion." *Scottish Mountaineering Club Journal,* 4 (1897), pp. 259-266.

"A Reverie." *Scottish Mountaineering Club Journal,* 5 (1898), pp. 93-102.

"Exploration in the Canadian Rockies; a search for Mount Brown and Mount Hooker." *Geographical Journal,* 13 (1899), pp. 337-355.

"Climbing in the Canadian Rocky Mountains." *Alpine Journal,* 19 (1899), pp. 252-267.

"Exploration in the Canadian Rocky Mountains." *Geographical Journal,* 17 (1901), pp. 252-267.

"Lofoten." *Alpine Journal,* 22 (1905), pp. 3-15.

"The Highest Climbs on Record." *Ibid.,* pp. 626-627.

"On the Canadian Rocky Mountains North of the Yellowhead Pass." *Alpine Journal,* 26 (1912), pp. 5-17.

"The Island of Skye." *Alpine Journal,* 32 (1920), pp. 163-165.

"Short Summary of Mountaineering in the Himalaya with Note on the Approaches to Everest." *Alpine Journal,* 33 (1921), pp. 295-303.

"The Ranges North of Mount Everest as Seen near the Kang La." *Ibid.,* pp. 303-305.

"Early Exploration of the Rocky Mountains." *Alpine Journal,* 33 (1921), pp. 319-322.

"Mount Everest Expedition: Organisation and Equipment." *Geographical Journal,* 57 (1921), pp. 272-273.

"The Mount Everest Expedition." *Alpine Journal,* 34 (1923), pp. 114-117.

"Old Memories: The Columbia Icefield." *Alpine Journal,* 35 (1923), pp. 240-242.

"Dreams." *Cairngorm Club Journal,* 13 (1932), pp. 59-69.

"John Mackenzie." *Scottish Mountaineering Club Journal,* 20 (1933), pp. 124-125.

"Independence." *Cairngorm Club Journal,* 15 (1939), pp. 15-17.

"Dreams." *Cairngorm Club Journal,* 15 (1943), pp. 205-215.

ACKNOWLEDGEMENTS

The photographs on the cover and on pp. vi-1 showing Collie in the chemical laboratory at University College, London c. 1910, and on pp. 9, 13, 16-17, 100-101, 171, together with pp. 156-157 showing 1. to r. John Mackenzie, John Campbell and Collie outside Sligachan Hotel in Skye c. 1930, appear by courtesy of Mrs Susan Benstead; on pp. 6, 49, 166-167 from the Collie Family Collection in the possession of Mrs Susan Benstead and Mrs Norah Holmes; on p. 161 from the *Union Magazine* of March 1908; on pp. 22-23 from T. Hope MacLachan, *A Climb in the Cuillin of Skye* (1896); on pp. 30, 43 from R. W. Clark, *A Pictorial History of Mountaineering* (1953), reproduced by permission of B. T. Batsford Ltd.; on p. 43, right-hand side, from W. Unsworth, *Tiger in the Snow: The Life and Adventures of A. F. Mummery* (1967), reproduced by permission of Victor Gollancz Ltd.; on pp. 36-37 showing a general view of the French Alps, Isère, by courtesy of the French Tourist Office, Montreal; on pp. 52-53 showing 1. to r. a Ghurka, Bruce and Mummery in camp at the side of the Rupal Glacier, Nanga Parbat, 1895, and on pp. 68-69, the Diama Pass, together with pp. 63, 79, and pp. 112-113 showing the Freshfield Group with Bush Pass on the r., together with pp. 118-119, 166-167 were taken by J. Norman Collie; on pp. 130-131 showing the village of Reine, Lofoten Islands, by courtesy of the Norwegian Information Service, New York; on pp. 142-143 showing Mount Robson, by courtesy of Canadian National; on pp. 126-127 by courtesy of the Alpine Club of Canada; on pp. 84-85 showing Baker, Sarbach and Collie outside Banff Springs Hotel, 1897, by courtesy of the Glenbow-Alberta Institute, Calgary; on p. 95 by courtesy of Mrs Charles E. Scribner.